GOURMET GAME

INTRODUCTION

When my father retired from tea-planting in Assam he returned to his roots in north-east Scotland, where his family variously farmed or distilled whisky. Cousin George Grant sent me a number of his special recipes for inclusion in this book, and most of these incorporate 'The Glenfarclas'.

Retirement to my father meant summers fishing the river Spey, and winters shooting on the hills and moors. On Sunday mornings he would clean his guns, sort tackle, and make any necessary repairs to these, and we, the females of the household, dealt with the game hung in the outhouse during the week. I say 'we', grandly but I really mean my mother, for my own participation in these chores was hardly onerous, and I remember my sister's contribution as nil, although this might possibly be a little unjust. I learned to pluck and clean all varieties of game but did my best to wriggle out of dealing with anything furry, although I was happy enough to share in all the eating that followed.

Our house looked across the Spey to a high ridge of pine-clad red rocks, which dropped to the winding Elgin Road and Craigellachie's famous silver-painted iron bridge built by Telford. The motto of the Grant clan is 'Stand Fast Craigellachie!' Craigellachie means literally 'the rock of alarm' and Grant clan territories stretched along the Spey valley from this village to a prominent rocky hill near Aviemore. It is really not so long ago that the Grants last went raiding into the 'fat lands o' Moray', which start widening into their fertile valley just across the river. Strathspey stretches between these two Craigellachies a distance of about 30km/20 miles. Alarm beacons used to be lit along its length whenever there was trouble, and by all accounts, the people of Strathspey were an unruly lot, with little regard for outsiders' laws or property.

Winter's ice always tried to seal the river, but never succeeded because of its fierce currents, and the waters rushed olive green and yellow, a jostling patchwork of ice breaking and re-forming in the eddies and by rocks. In summer the river returned to its inscrutable peat-brown, the colour of the malt whisky distilled along the valley. The most poignant debris washed up by its waters were the kelts, salmon which had made their journey to spawn in the river's high rushes, and then died. Their spent bodies littered spring ice floes and sandbanks, and the rotting corpses were irresistible temptation to the village dogs.

CONTENTS

First published in Great Britain in 1989 by
Barrie & Jenkins Ltd
289 Westbourne Grove, London W11 2QA

British Library Cataloguing in Publication Data
Scott, Philippa, *1946-*
    Gourmet game.
    1. Food: Game dishes. – Recipes
    I. Title
    641.6'91

ISBN 0 7126 2147 4

Designed by Patrick McLeavey
Typeset by SX Composing Ltd
Colour separation by York House
Printed and bound in Great Britain by Cowells of Ipswich

GOURMET GAME

RECIPES AND ANECDOTES FROM AROUND THE WORLD

PHILIPPA SCOTT

ILLUSTRATIONS BY FRANCESCA PELIZZOLI

BARRIE & JENKINS
LONDON

The prospect of rolling in these was a stronger pull than the threat of an inevitable beating and bath to follow.

Nostalgia is, of course, a seductive indulgence. I have palate-watering memories of wild raspberry feasts picked from the back of a grazing pony, a low-slung, short, fat, stubborn Shetland. Her bare back also provided a slippery perch for raiding the gean trees. The fruits, bitter-tasting wild cherries, have a flavour not far from that of morellos, and the leaves turn a vivid crimson in autumn. Birds love these little fruit, and it was always a race to catch the moment when the cherries were ripe enough to eat, but the birds had not got to them first. The birds usually won.

We pulled cranberries and blueberries among the silver birches as their leaves turned yellow. These berries grew together in neighbourly profusion on low bushes bedded in peat, heather and springy sphagnum moss that tossed little dried leaves, twigs and tiny caterpillars down the tops of our wellington boots as we moved around with baskets and bowls. Every bowl in the house was commandeered for the picking, usually a Sunday job. Scottish cranberries are smaller and sharper-tasting than any I have since bought in London, and they provided tart sauces as accompaniments for winter pheasant and grouse, delicious jellies and jams and meringue-topped open pies.

There were abundant harvests of wild mushrooms. In those days the people of the village did not care to eat these, and our habit of doing so was regarded with slight concern. The Heather Isle is not an island but a stretch of uncultivated, scrubby land along the river, where ponies and cattle grazed, Glasgow Boy Scouts camped once

a year and herons fished for frogs in the pool which provided spring frogspawn for a series of jars ranged along the windows in school. It was a prime source for field mushrooms, and I knew a beech wood where the golden, delectable trumpets of chanterelles were so abundant that you could smell the spot before it was visible. To reach this hidden, golden treasure trove, pick and be home in time for high tea, took most of a day spent scrambling across country, but the reward was generous, worth all the scraped knees and bramble grazes.

Because of this way of life many of our meals consisted of caught and hunted food: salmon, seatrout, hare (no rabbit, it was the time of myxamatosis and the rabbit population had been almost wiped out by that foul and efficient infection), duck, pheasant, partridge and grouse. Venison appeared occasionally. In winter, to ring the changes, there was some of summer's catch of salmon, which had been smoked and was succulent and moist, better than any plastic-wrapped packages (for which, today, I am nevertheless deeply appreciative). Surplus salmon was weighed, packed in bags of rush matting and sent straight to London on the evening train, to be sold next morning.

'Then' is far from 'now', but it explains some of my early-formed tastes and a preference for wild meat. To someone once heard to mutter, 'Not salmon again', or even to whinge, 'Couldn't we have chicken for a change', divine retribution falls in the form of city life and supermarkets. Still, city shopping today offers a wide choice of ingredients for interesting cooking and eating, and the availability of products from every part of the globe. London's Portobello market on my doorstep takes me round the world and back on every visit, even if I am hunting nothing more exotic than tinned cat food.

When you live in a village everybody knows all there is to know about you, and a little more besides. In a city, less so. When people asked the question 'What do you do/do you work/what are you up to now?' depending on our degree of acquaintance or friendship, and I replied, according to whatever it happened to be at the time, 'carpet dealer/Islamic textile specialist/illustrator/transcontinental Land Rover driver', the response was usually polite, or interested, or puzzled. Never before embarking on this book did I hear 'Ugh!'

Not from everyone, of course. Many were enthusiastic, helpful; one friend offered to introduce me to his aunt in Paris who serves narwhal and polar bear steaks for lunch, although, he hastened to add, she does not serve these every day. Incidentally, I read somewhere that polar bear liver contains such a high concentration of vitamin A that it can prove fatal. You turn orange as you die. *Nota Bene.*

The reaction to the topic of game is varied and definite; strongly flavoured indeed, like game itself. What concerns me is that, as meat eaters, we should have consideration both for ourselves as to the quality of our food, and for the animals which are raised and killed to feed us. Personally, I don't want to eat something which has lived and died in conditions of torture, and I neither want, nor need, to eat meat every day or at every meal. For people like me game is an answer, and I am very happy indeed to eat farm-raised game, the earliest and truest form of free-range farming. Does 'farmed game' sound like a contradiction in terms? Consider.

Stress raises the level of adrenalin in the blood, which depletes the store of glycogen in muscle cells. In terms of meat this means that if an animal suffers stress for any length of time before death, changes take place in the biochemistry of the blood and muscle which affect the taste and keeping quality of the meat. This increases the acidity of the meat, and the same sequence of protein breakdown happens whatever the cause of stress, whether the animal is trapped, wounded, hunted for a long period, or loaded on to trucks to be taken to a slaughterhouse.

In this respect, farmed deer and wild boar have the preferred exit, as the animal is shot in its home paddock, an event which often passes barely noticed by the rest of the herd. Wild boar, re-introduced into Britain some years ago, have to be kept under special licence. When I was told this I said brightly, 'Oh, you mean like Pigling Bland and the Black Berkshire?' Far from it. It means that they are subject to the specifications of the Dangerous Wild Animals Act, which applies equally to tigers and wolves, not at all Beatrix Potter. The strict rules of this Act totally preclude any possibility of abattoir death.

Domestication means more than simple tameness. In winter red deer can become so tame that they will take fodder from the hand of someone who regularly puts out fodder for them; but they are not domesticated animals, they have not been selectively bred away from the state which enables them to survive in the wild.

The earliest record of deer farming is from approximately three thousand years ago in China, comparatively recent in terms of animal husbandry and domestication. Deer antlers and bones have been found in many very ancient sites and excavations; but despite their ancient and important role in the survival and evolution of humanity, deer have not been turned into high-yield, docile production machines which could not exist in their present state without man. Deer have escaped this end, unlike sheep and cattle. Deer parks have existed for thousands of years, but deer remain wild game. Humans have been meateaters for a very long time; thousands of years passed before any animals were domesticated. Early cave paintings illustrate the importance of our ancestors' relationship with wild animals, in terms of survival and in terms of sacred interdependence. Lean, wild shapes, the ancestors of today's lumbering cattle, are among the mysterious and beautiful forms painted on the walls of Lascaux, and on other sheltered rock faces the world over.

Animal meat and fat were especially important in a diet where weather conditions were such that reliance on berries, plants, roots and seeds was insufficient. Every part of the animal killed was used to nourish and shelter, nothing was wasted. The Indians of North America, whose traditional way of life revolved so intimately around nature and hunting, term this 'the giveaway'. That is an approximation of their word; nobody is suggesting that an animal (or plant) has committed suicide or offered itself as a voluntary sacrifice with altruistic intention. But in considering that it has given away its life so that we might live, there is both appreciation and respect, a realistic acceptance of the cycle of life and death understood by people who live close to nature, and are dependent on nature. That is vastly different from excessive sentimentality and squeamishness to which city living makes us prone.

Game, then, means undomesticated animals and birds, those which have not been genetically engineered to become walking larders. Some of our farmyard familiars return very quickly to a feral type. A good example of this is the razorback hog of America, the domestic pig which has reverted to an earlier type through living and breeding in a wild state. In this case selective breeding has worked backwards: a slow, fat porker would have little chance of escaping predators long enough to breed more slow, fat porkers; but fierce, fast wild pigs are not to be trifled with. These wild pigs are game in the same sense as traditional wild boar.

Not many rabbits which appear on our tables today have led a wild life, and there is, of course, a difference in flavour between wild and hutch rabbits. Quail have been reared for the table (and, pugnacious little creatures, for quail fighting) for centuries. Even though they are raised domestically in many countries they have escaped the unforgivable treatment of domestic chickens, they are not battery-farmed and mutilated. By nature quail are migratory birds, and in California, for example, the quail-shooting season is keenly anticipated. Recipes for the wild and the farm-raised are basically the same; only a little commonsense adaptation is required. Farmyard duck and geese are much fatter than the wild ones, and should be treated accordingly. Similarly, a favourite recipe for beef can be adapted to venison.

Shooting and fishing seasons take into consideration the breeding cycles, when the animals are legally protected and out of bounds, and the end of summer, when they are as plump as they are likely to be, ready to face the harsh conditions of winter. There are different hunting seasons and restrictions for different species, and these vary from country to country. Farmed game, however, is available all year round; there is no closed season. Game for sale should be labelled, stating whether it is wild or farm-reared, and this also applies to farmed trout and salmon. In the case of the fishes, I would always prefer the wild to the farmed, both for the superior flavour and for the way they have lived.

In most countries game is considered normal fare, and if it is available it is taken for granted that you eat it. The Americans are prepared to try most things, game for anything, you might say, from squirrel and porcupine, through beavers and bears, to the giant moose. They cook them in a variety of ways, enjoy them and don't attach any particular snobbery to one type or another. There is no special reverence for game in European countries, where it is cooked, eaten and relished in all manner of ways. Although the Italian passion for little songbirds is hard to consider sporting, I suppose it could be argued that it is a continuation of the Roman taste for millet-fattened finches (and dormice too, I'm afraid) as a delicacy.

In Rajasthan, where the people are Hindu and do not eat beef, wild boar and venison used to be an important part of all feasts, and it still is when, for instance, there is a grand or noble wedding. I was lucky enough to be in Udaipur when there was such a wedding, and because of my interest and the kindness of my friends, I was allowed to make a perfect nuisance of myself hanging around in the palace kitchens, from the moment when the deer and wild boar arrived, dead but otherwise intact, throughout the various processes of preparation which led up to the banquets. I participated fully in the feasting, and returned to London with sheaves of colourfully spattered notes.

Thomas Carlyle was convinced that it was the poachers of France who fuelled the citizens' grumblings which led to the Revolution, and certainly, one of the first acts passed by the revolutionaries was the dismantling of the game laws. In all countries there were harsh and savage punishments for what landowners considered poaching, and country people considered their right. In Britain, perhaps more than other countries, there lingers an attitude that certain meats (pheasant, venison and grouse particularly) are daring, extravagant, definitely not everyday food. There is a certain snobbery and mystique attached to these, and in some quarters it is considered shocking . . . sacrilegous even . . . to stray from traditional roasting methods, whatever the condition of the meat. This attitude does not extend to rabbit, hare or duck, and it may be related to the fact that pheasant is not indigenous to Britain; it was always specially raised by gamekeepers, even as today, and it was not until the eighteenth century that the pheasant became a normal wild inhabitant of the countryside.

Trophy hunting (for the edible and inedible), and all sorts of hunting, reached exaggerated proportions in the nineteenth century, the rising popularity of grouse moors and deer stalking culminating in the savagery of the Highland Clearances, when small crofters were turned off their land to make way for the fashionable sporting Highland Scotland of the Victorian era. It was with some bitterness, indeed, that the history of the Clearances was dinned into me at school, and the evidence was on the hillsides all around: little tumbledown bothies, crumbling patchworks of dykes. I have no doubt this made me all the more sensitive to Rajasthan when I go to Udaipur. There the hillsides are dotted with shooting boxes, impotent sentinels standing guard over the ghosts of forests-that-used-to-be, now sun-parched scrub. In India, as everwhere else, the country people have always taken the forests and jungles for granted, a constant source of firewood and wildlife. But after independence in 1947 the government 'relieved' the royal families of India of many things, including land, and many forests were cut for instant cash. Replanting has been far down on the list of priorities.

The dubious reputation sometimes attributed to game meat is probably a consequence of serving meat which was hunted for antler size (meat therefore of secondary importance, and as a result mishandled), or meat which was overhung, or just badly cooked. People who were not brought up with game as a normal part of their diet sometimes have hesitation about trying it, for these reasons, and expect dried-out, pungent meat.

Game meats need sensitivity in their cooking. Factors such as age, type and condition are all important in deciding the cooking method. Not all meats, or cuts, require lengthy cooking. Roasted game birds take very little time, and an escalope of farm-raised venison, unstressfully culled at two years, prime and tender, beaten thin between two layers of greaseproof paper and quickly seared, takes only minutes to reach delicious perfection.

The calorie content is dependent on the recipe and its additional ingredients. Game meat is healthy meat, low in fat, and care must be taken in the cooking to make sure that it remains succulent. Traditionally this has been done by adding butter, cream or rich sauces, and larding with fat. Delicious; yet if you want to profit from its low cholesterol factor, it is possible to enjoy game without additional fatty ingredients, and at the same time to take full advantage of its wholesome protein in tasty recipes. For this reason, I have included a wide and varied selection of recipes, and I hope there are dishes to suit all palates, occasions and desires.

There are people who profess to dislike game because of its strong and distinctive flavour. Among today's chickens, only farmyard and free range birds have any real taste; the commercially battery-raised chickens have no flavour without the addition of seasonings, herbs, sauces and the like. You might as well use soya protein: it will taste the same, and it will be hormone-free and stress-free. After such a diet of relatively bland-tasting meat, game certainly makes the tastebuds sit up and pay attention.

The British custom of hanging meat serves both to tenderize it and bring out this gamey aspect of its taste. Even beef is hung for these same reasons. There are some who do not consider pheasant ready to eat until the bird's body drops off the neck as it hangs (obviously the hang-them-by-the-neck-school). Too high for my taste, and not necessary. There are other ways of tenderizing, using various marinades and juices. In hot countries there is no question of hanging any meat: it would be rotten and fly-blown and definitely not a tempting culinary prospect.

As part of our increased attention to health and environmental issues, meat, particularly red meat, has received a certain amount of criticism. The best advice to omnivores is to eat the meat from animals that were fit and healthy in their lifetimes. Game has much to recommend it, as it comes from free-ranging, lean and healthy animals which have not been pumped full of antibiotics as are domestic animals.

On the subject of cholesterol, and lean and fat meats, studies have been made of the Navaho and Inuit (Eskimo) people, both of whom ingest huge quantities of animal fats, and yet who show little or no cholesterol build-up. The troubles start when animal fat is combined with carbohydrate, and when the tension and pressure of modern city life are added to this, the stage is set for problems. Fat on its own is not the culprit; it is the way in which we combine our food intake and the mental and emotional state we are in when we try to digest it. Studies have been made on ideal ways of combining foods, and it is a good idea for all of us be aware of these patterns. There are also a number of diets which are based on a high protein and low carbohydrate intake, and they date back to the nineteenth century and the experience of a certain Mr Banting. The best known of these modern diets are the Scarsdale diet, the Atkins diet, the drinking man's diet, and the air force diet. These are all aimed at losing weight by eliminating carbohydrates and sending the body into an abnormal condition called ketosis. This is not what I am advocating, and is not the point of this book.

In 1906 a young Harvard anthropologist named Viljamur Stefansson went to the Arctic with the Leffingwell-Mikkelson expedition. Plans miscarried and Stefansson was left to spend an Arctic winter with the Inuit. He must have faced this prospect with mixed excitement, I imagine, because of the rich research opportunity it afforded, and fears that he might not survive long enough to take advantage of the chance. The Inuit diet was fish, washed down with the water in which the fish had been briefly stewed. Stefansson tried to adapt this to his taste, by grilling the fish, but rapidly succumbed to dizziness and all the symptoms of malnutrition, and he realised that on this highly restricted diet the body needs the nutrients in the cooking water, including the fats, as well as the protein of the fish flesh. He adjust to the Inuit diet and survived in good health. Further experients and research continued in future expeditions, showing that the hunters' diet – the fish they could catch, the meat they could kill, the water they could find, mixed with whatever wild berries and herbs and plants were available – was sufficient to maintain health, as long as the natural oil and fat were included. Without this they fell ill.

Protein-based diets, and diets based on the study of correct combinations of food are descendants of these researches. Nutritional supplements such as cod-liver oil and salmon oil are easily available to those who want to take them, though why anyone would prefer salmon oil capsules to a meal of that delicious fish is beyond my understanding! Although red meat has received quite a lot of criticism in recent years, it would seem that under extreme conditions, such as Eskimo life, a diet incorporating every element of the meat, including the fat and oil available, and of course fresh water, can be adequate. No doubt the Inuit, who are used to this, fare better than someone from a different culture and background who is suddenly confronted with having to exist on such a diet.

To the rest of us, who have a vast choice of foodstuffs available to us if we live in one of the larger cities, consideration should be given to the ways we combine these, and this history of the foodstuffs before they reach the shops or our plates. In this respect game has much to recommend it, but it also offers a vastly superior flavour. I would rather eat roe-deer venison than lamb, pheasant than the finest chicken. In the water-fowl family, my taste concurs with that of Thomas Venner, who wrote in 1628, in his *Via recta ad vitam longam* (The Straight Way to a Long Life), '. . . teal, for pleasantness and wholesomenesse of meat, exalteth all other waterfowle.' Ernest Hemingway was another who endorsed Venner's feelings about this small duck, and before him John James Audubon, the great naturalist and artist, who arrived in America in 1803 and recorded the wealth of animal and bird life he found there in his *Birds of America* and *The Viviparous Quadrupeds of North America*, wrote of the blue-winged teal, '. . . so tender and savoury is its flesh that it would quickly put the merits of the widely-celebrated canvas-backed duck in the shade.' However, Audubon saved his greatest praise for the woodcock.

Travel, and our eating habits, illustrate recent changes in lifestyle. Travel has become a normal part of life, and tastes in eating have also changed. The requirements for maintaining our bodies within this rapidly changing world with its constant stresses and challenges have also contributed to new eating habits. Our tastes are more international. This is clear from reading a menu in any fashionable restaurant, or from dishes served at dinner parties at home. It is evident from high street supermarkets and delicatessen-prepared dishes, from frozen dinners, ethnic restaurants everywhere, and wholefood and vegetarian suppliers and caterers. International chefs advise us on television, on radio, in newspapers and books. There are many schools of cooking, and you may study the subject at home with video series. The world is our culinary oyster, whether there is an R in the month or not.

National palates also give preference to certain tastes: and the Moroccan recipe of pigeon cooked with almonds, cinnamon and sugar in their famous pie, the *bistela*, has a different balance and emphasis from a French dish of pheasant cooked with cream, apples and Calvados; or Georgian pheasant simmered in green tea, sweet wine, muscat grapes, the juice of blood oranges and peeled (bravo!) walnuts; or indeed, a Greek dish where the birds are stuffed with cracked coriander seeds and olives, and laid on twigs of rosemary and thyme, to cook slowly with lemon juice, garlic and olive oil. In Persia a duck might be cooked with pomegranate juice and pounded walnuts; in France with baby turnips and dry white wine. In Rajasthan plump partridges might be lightly marinated in yoghurt and lime juice, then stuffed with whole spices and grilled very slowly with frequent basting; but in Spain the same birds might be cooked with herbs in a rich sauce of unsweetened chocolate (don't think of it as chocolate), reminding us of the tastes the conquistadores brought back from the Americas.

These recipes, and the rest in this book, have come from friends, family and years of dedicated greed, eating my way through many countries. There are recipes which have evolved from something read in a magazine or book, and a few I have resisted tampering with, and I thank the writers who collected and published these recipes so that the rest of us might enjoy them. A beautiful dish is like a *caravanserai*, it is neither the beginning nor the end of the journey, but it offers something nourishing, refreshing, exciting, the opportunity of lively and shared exchange. Desert hospitality is justly famous for requiring that a stranger be fed, and hospitality must be honoured, never abused.

As the ingredients vary according to the type and diet of the animal, so the seasonings and spices vary depending on their shelf life, and the soil, climate and weather of their growing time. The unlisted magical ingredient in any recipe is the personality and palate of the cook, and it is well known that two people can make the same dish in a similar way and it will differ, and that the same person can make the same dish time and again, and it can be subtly different each time.

Because of these regional variations, I have given two recipes for Moroccan *bistela*, one using chicken or squab, which will closely reproduce the Moroccan flavour, and the second a recipe which I have evolved out of the first, through using native British dark-fleshed wood pigeons. This second is a gamier version, probably closer to a medieval game pie than to its Moroccan inspiration. They are both delicious and, after all, that is what cooking and eating is about. It is never a static or rigid process.

The point is to enjoy. Don't be afraid to experiment, to vary, to improvise. Most potential or impending disasters can be saved somehow, and your appreciative guests will probably never know. There are, naturally, instances where my informal attitude would not be appropriate or tolerable. For example, my mother taught Cordon Bleu cookery at the Tante Marie School, and in that temple of professionalism everything has to be 'just so'.

However, I am neither a professional cook nor a famous chef. In my own life, and in my own kitchen, cooking for friends, the whole experience functions on the pleasure principle, enjoyment shared. That principle is the intention and statement of this book.

NOTE ON MEASUREMENTS

In the recipes that follow, weights of birds and other creatures that are given are intended only as a rough guide. Obviously you will be making that dish with birds of whatever weight you have; but if the weight is much larger or smaller than that given, at least you will be warned that you should scale the other ingredients up or down to suit. Weight of whole animals are given before plucking, skinning or drawing; this of course does not apply to joints of meat from larger animals.

For the sake of giving round numbers, metric weights are about 10 per cent larger than their imperial equivalents. In most recipes that will make no practical difference; but in the more complicated sauces etc. it is wise to use only metric or only imperial measurements throughout. Spoon measurements are level unless otherwise stated.

American measures are given following the metric and imperial weights. A glossary is included for any cookery terms or ingredients that might be unfamiliar to American cooks.

THE GAME COOK'S KITCHEN

Like many people, I find an enormous gap between what I would like to have and what I do have. That applies to my kitchen. In an ideal world, my kitchen would be spacious, practical and serene; only ingredients in constant use would be stored there. The atmosphere of calm would be enhanced by displays of beautiful plates and dishes, a wonderful sound system, a comfy armchair near the bookshelves, and a discreet, silent assistant, whose pleasure was to weep over the chopped onions for me. There would be adjacent cold pantries and larders with shelves I could reach without difficulty, laden with jars, tins, utensils and anything which was functional but not aesthetically pleasing. French cheeses would be stored here at a perfect temperature, as would fruit, vegetables and fresh produce, and there would be a game larder and deep freeze. Nothing unusual or original in that, but tradition often has its roots in the truly functional.

What I have, in fact, is a small London flat, where the kitchen is a narrow slice off my bedroom, storage is minimal and definitely inadequate, and every corner and shelf overflows. I have a large fridge which we call 'the bodysnatcher', and this serves as my larder. When a kind friend gives me a brace of pheasants, I remove a shelf from the bodysnatcher, rearrange the contents (which are always well wrapped) and hang the birds inside. It's not ideal, but if I hang them in the flat they will be too warm, and anyway the cats will go berserk with such temptation; alternatively if I hang them outside a window in London, invader cats will destroy them if a two-legged thief doesn't take them first.

Why don't I give them to one of our excellent local butchers? Because it is a simple job to pluck and clean a brace of birds, one I can do quickly and well. The exception would be in the case of a bird hit by a car and retrieved. Mindful of my friend John Whitehead's experience, I would take such a bird to the butcher. John did so, and warned his wife Rebecca that their pheasant would be a bit mangled, so she should be prepared to casserole it. Imagine their delight when he unwrapped a beautiful bird, which, it turned out, even had pellets of shot in it!

At the end of the day, it comes down to individual convenience and personal preference.

UTENSILS

Nothing exotic is required in the line of tools. A meat saw, meat cleaver, a set of very sharp knives of various sizes, a pair of good kitchen scissors, perhaps some poultry shears, larding needles, trussing twine and needles, skewers, and the rest of one's normal *batterie* of wooden spoons, chopping boards and so on. Pots and pans which conduct heat evenly, such as Dutch oven type pots with wire racks inside, made of cast iron with close-fitting lids, or of heavy earthenware, are ideal for game. Kitchen foil is the game cook's blessing of this century.

STOCK

I have a mania about stock, rather like Linus's comfort blanket: I am unhappy if I do not have good home-made stock constantly available. This whim is easy to pander to, and I can freeze it in containers and even in ice-cube trays for small quantities to zip up the flavour of vegetables or a sauce. None of the sprinkle-a-cube stuff is ever as good as your own, so why bother with anything else?

GAME STOCK

The basis for this is the carcass (or carcasses) of whichever game birds you have, together with the scalded feet, and cleaned giblets.

500g/1 lb veal bones, with marrow	*2 celery sticks, chopped*	*2 bouquet garnis*	*game carcasses, feet and giblets*
1 large onion, sliced	*250g/½ lb/2 cups carrots, chopped*	*salt and black peppercorns*	*cold water*

Cover the ingredients with cold water, bring slowly to boiling point, and remove any scum from the surface. Cover the pan with a tight-fitting lid and simmer over the lowest possible heat for about 4 hours to extract all the flavour from the bones. Top up with hot water if the level of the liquid should fall below the other ingredients. Strain the stock into a large bowl, through a fine sieve or muslin.

Leave it to settle. If you are going to use it immediately, the fat will have to be removed. As the stock cools, the fat will rise to the surface. It can be removed by drawing absorbent kitchen paper over it. If the stock is not required immediately, leave the fat to settle in a surface layer which can be easily lifted off later. If it is kept in the fridge, it should be boiled up every two days to ensure freshness. If frozen, it can be kept for up to two months. In this case, it is a good idea to concentrate it before freezing. This is done by boiling over high heat.

Makes 1l/2½ pints/5 cups of stock

MARINADES

There are three reasons for marinating meat. One is to flavour the meat with the ingredients of the marinade, herbs, spices and wine. Sometimes the marinade is included in the cooking process, for basting, or incorporated in the cooking liquid and sauce. Another reason for marinating is to render meat which is tough or of questionable age more juicy, for which purpose the marinade incorporates oil. Another is to make meat more tender, and this is done by including an acid such as lemon juice or vinegar.

Wine has a similar though less drastic effect. In eastern countries a mixture which includes yoghurt and papaya or green mango is used for tenderizing. Certain natural enzymes, especially the powerful ones found in these and other fruits such as figs and pineapples - especially when slightly unripe – break down the proteins in meat. Such mixtures can act so quickly that if left too long, the meat will be like cotton wool: be careful. A cooked marinade relying on acid alone for its effect is another useful means of tenderizing tough old meat.

GENERAL MARINADE

Adjust this one to your taste and requirements; the basic recipe is given here. Red wine suits venison, pigeons and some pheasant recipes. White wine suits guinea fowl, quail, and also pheasants. Wild boar does well with either. Wine vinegar will make the marinade stronger, and you can substitute vinegar for wine, or use them together. Other marinade recipes can be found on page 150.

150 ml/5 fl oz/²/₃ cup olive oil	*1 carrot, chopped*	*6 black peppercorns, cracked*	*parsley and thyme, chopped*
150 ml/5 fl oz/²/₃ cup red or white wine	*2 sticks of celery, chopped*	*6 juniper berries, crushed*	
1 onion, chopped	*2 cloves of garlic, crushed*	*1 bay leaf*	

Add the meat to this mixture, and turn it from time to time; 12 hours is usually long enough to marinate any meat, unless it is very old or very tough, in which case you may need to marinate it in a cold place for 2 or 3 days.
Enough for 1 kg/2 lb meat

BIRDS OF FIELD, WOOD AND MOOR

PHEASANT

The pheasant is probably the most familiar game bird, and yet it has been so for a comparatively brief time. There are various types of pheasant, all indigenous to Asia, and these range from the glorious Golden pheasant of China, kept more for its plumage than its flesh, to the common pheasant we are all familiar with. Legend – and its Latin name, *Phasianus colchicus* – tell how the Argonauts first encountered this bird on their travels to the River Phasis in Colchis on the eastern shore of the Black Sea. The Greeks then introduced it to Rome, whence it travelled across Europe with the Roman legions as part of their living larder. Edible snails and roe deer also came to Britain in this way. In Britain pheasant have always been raised by gamekeepers, and only in the last couple of centuries have they flown freely to become a part of the native countryside. Pheasant shooting reached the summit of fashion in the nineteenth century.

A young, plump juicy bird in its prime is delicious roasted in a traditional manner, but if it fails on any of these points it should be enjoyed in another form. The hen bird provides meat that is moister and more delicately flavoured than that of the cock, and it is slightly smaller. A brace of pheasants invariably consists of a cock and a hen, and, of course, their cooking times, and their meat, will vary slightly. If they are to be cooked together try to make sure they are, at least, the same size.

ROAST PHEASANT

There are many favourite ways of roasting pheasant. In my part of north-east Scotland it was sometimes done to include a little sprig of heather between the barding layers, but I would not swear that this adds anything to the flavour. Our favourite stuffing was one made of good oatmeal, tasty dripping from a roast, onions, cloves and herbs. A Scots' version of bread sauce? There were also local sausages filled with this mixture, and known as Mealie Jimmies.

Pheasant is best cooked upside down, or on its side. It requires frequent turning and basting so that the breast meat doesn't dry out, as this is thinner meat than the thighs and so cooks more quickly. Another way of counteracting dryness is to stuff something moist underneath the skin, such as bacon, fruit or cream cheese. The recipe given on page 24 using Roquefort cheese and leeks is delicious.

One of my few parsimonious habits is to hoard butter wrappers. I never throw these away until they have served me one last time, either as covers for the first part of the roasting time of any bird, or for buttering a dish, or to lay on top of rice as it cooks. Little bacon rolls cooked beside the pheasant (or any other game bird) flavour the basting fat and make a tasty accompaniment.

Any stuffing should be included in the weight of the bird, and it should be well barded or constantly basted and turned. To bard, smear the bird with butter, grind on some black pepper, and then tie a broad slice of bacon fat to cover the breast. An alternative method is to cover the buttered breast with a blanched vine leaf before tying the bard. If you prefer to insert some succulent and moisture-giving ingredient under the skin, do this before barding. Preheat the oven to 220°C/425°F/gas 7.

Melt butter, dripping or oil in a pan. Brown the birds all over in this for 5 to 10 minutes, then transfer them with the fat to a roasting pan. Roast unbarded birds on their side, or upside down with plenty of hot fat poured over them. Keep basting and turning. Small pheasants weighing about 600 g/1 ¼ lb will need 20 to 25 minutes, depending how pink you like the meat. Add 15 minutes or so for larger birds of about 1.3 kg/2 ½ lb. Pheasants are best eaten still pink. If overcooked their flesh is less succulent. Allow 1 pheasant per 2-4 people, depending on size.

It is important to rest the pheasant in a cooling oven, just as you would a chicken, so at the end of this time turn the oven off and open the door. Let it sit for a minimum of 10 minutes. If you do not rest the pheasant, it will not finish cooking, and it will be difficult to carve.

PHEASANT COCK-A-LEEKIE

This is an old favourite, for which different people have different versions. This is the one I grew up knowing. Some people use prunes instead of barley – but there is an interesting recipe with prunes later in this chapter.

1 largish pheasant, about 1.3 kg/2½ lb	*2.5l/4 pints/2½ quarts good home-made stock*	*generous handful of barley, well soaked*	*squeeze of lemon juice (optional)*
1.5 kg/3 lb leeks		*salt and black pepper*	

Wash and trim the leeks well. Make sure no grit or earth is caught between the leaves. Slice them, then simmer everything together until the pheasant is tender, 40 minutes or more, and the barley is chewable.

Adjust the seasonings. Serve each bowlful with a piece of bird, and a good mixture of barley and leeks. I like lots of pepper; and sometimes a squeeze of lemon.
Serves 4

PHEASANT WITH LEMON GRASS

Lemon grass, or citronella, is used a great deal in South-East Asian cooking. It has
a very distinctive flavour, and is particularly delicious with birds and seafood.

*1 large pheasant, about
    1.5 kg/3 lb
4 Petit Suisse cheeses
1 blade of lemon grass,
    shredded*

*1 clover of garlic
black pepper
fresh thyme
120 g/4 oz/⅔ cup hazel
    or other nuts,*

*chopped (optional)
250 g/8 oz/1⅓ cups
    leeks, chopped
    (optional)
8 rashers of bacon*

*250 g/8 oz/½ lb vine
    leaves, drained and
    washed if packet, or
    quickly blanched if
    fresh*

Preheat the over to 240°C/475°F/gas 9. Mash the
cream cheese and lemon grass. Crush the garlic
and add this. Grind some black pepper, and
crush some thyme into the mixture. Carefully
spread this under the skin of the pheasant. Any
extra can be mixed into a stuffing if you want
one, using the chopped nuts and leeks.

Cover the breast of the bird with a criss-cross
lattice of bacon, then wrap it securely in the vine
leaves, using thin string to secure these in place.
Wrap the whole package in foil, and roast in the
oven for 1 hour.
Serves 4

MOROCCAN PRUNE TAGINE

A dish like this tagine is
mentioned in a medieval
Arab manuscript of 1204,
the *Kitab al-Wusla il al-
Habib*.

Here is a version of a Moroccan fruit tagine made with prunes. Any fruit can be
used for this dish; quinces are especially delicious.

*1 pheasant or guinea
    fowl, about 1 kg/2 lb
3 onions, 1 sliced and 2
    finely chopped*

*¼ teaspoon powdered
    saffron
½ teaspoon crushed fresh
    ginger, or ginger
    paste*

*salt and black pepper
stock or water to cover
    bird
500 g/1 lb/5 cups*

*prunes, soaked
overnight and drained*

Wash the bird and put it in a large pan with the
sliced onions. Add the spices and seasonings,
cover it with stock or water and simmer it gently
until the bird is almost tender, about 40 minutes.
    Add the finely chopped onions and continue

to simmer gently. When the bird is fully tender,
add the prunes and continue cooking, with the
pan uncovered, until the prunes are soft and the
sauce is reduced. Serve with rice or couscous.
Serves 4-6

SCANDINAVIAN ROAST PHEASANT STUFFED WITH GRAPES

1 large pheasant, about
  1.5 kg/3 lb
1-2 tablespoons butter

salt and black pepper
250 g/8 oz/1½ cups
  grapes

flour for gravy
150 ml/5 fl oz/⅔ cup
  stock or water

150 ml/5 fl oz/⅔ cup
  dry white wine

Rinse the pheasant, dry it thoroughly and rub a little of the butter and some salt and pepper well into the skin.

Rinse the grapes; if they have seeds, you may prefer to remove these. I think it is worth the effort, and is easily done with the looped end of a hair grip. Preheat the oven to 180°C/350°F/gas 4.

Stuff the bird with grapes, sew it up and truss it. Melt the remaining butter in a roasting pan, and put the bird on the oven breast down, first on one side then on the other, to brown. After 20 minutes put it breast up in the pan and cover the breast with buttered paper (or old butter wrap-per). Roast for another 40 minutes, but take care not to overcook it.

When the bird is done, let it rest in a warm place while you make the gravy. Pour off any excess fat from the roasting tin, and scrape the brown residue loose. Stir in a little flour, and when this has been well incorporated, pour the stock or water into the pan. Let the mixture cook over a low heat to a smooth consistency, then add the white wine, and reduce again until slightly thickened. Carve the bird and arrange it on a warm serving dish. Serve the sauce separately.
Serves 4

The ancient Chinese and Egyptians favoured pigeons, but Queen Victoria's favourite game bird was a pheasant stuffed with chopped truffles and foie gras, and braised in a little Maderia. Sounds delicious.

CIRCASSIAN BIRDS

During the Ottoman Empire, the Circassians were renowned for both the beauty and for the culinary skills of their women. This is a recipe usually made today with chicken, and a favourite Turkish buffet dish. The ingredients are not unlike (dare I say this?) a superior bread sauce . . . and as an accompaniment to pheasant, utterly delicious. The sauce is equally good with cold leftover fowl.

2 pheasant, each about 1 kg/2 lb
1 onion stuck with a couple of cloves
celery stalks
sprig of thyme
salt and black pepper
2 slices of dry white bread, crusts removed
250 g/8 oz/1/3 cups walnuts, ground
1 clove of garlic, crushed
2 teaspoons paprika dissolved in 2 teaspoons walnut oil

Take the flesh off the birds. Put the carcasses in a saucepan with water. Bring to the boil, then skim. Add the onion, celery, thyme, salt and pepper, and simmer for 30 minutes. Add the flesh of the birds and simmer until tender, about another 50 minutes.

Soak the bread in a little of the stock and mash or blend it to a paste. Mix this in a small saucepan with the walnuts, and add the garlic and enough stock to make it like a thick porridge. Cook it for a few minutes. Shred the pheasant meat and mix it well with two-thirds of the sauce. Spread it on a serving dish and mask with the rest of the sauce. Dribble the paprica in oil over this as a garnish. Serve hot, warm or cold.
Serves 6

PHEASANT WITH CREAM

1 large pheasant, about 1.5 kg/3 lb
1 clove of garlic, crushed
1 teaspoon rosemary
1 teaspoon sage
120 g/4 oz/1/4 lb belly of pork or fatty bacon
1 teaspoon dry mustard
1 tablespoon Worcestershire sauce
250 ml/8 fl oz/1 cup single cream
2 tablespoons cognac
1 teaspoon cornflour (optional)
salt and pepper

Preheat the oven to 180°C/350°F/gas 4. Rub the bird with a mixture of crushed garlic, rosemary and sage. Bard the breast with slices of pork or bacon. Roast it, covered, in the oven for about 1 hour, then remove the lid and allow the bird to brown for another 30 minutes.

Take the bird out of the pan but keep it warm, and remove the slices of bacon or pork. Strain the juice from the pan into a saucepan. Add the mustard, Worcestershire sauce and cream. Ignite the cognac and pour it into the pan. Heat the sauce gently, without boiling, for a few minutes. If it seems too liquid, thicken it with cornflour which has been mixed to a smooth paste with a little water. Season with salt and pepper.

Cut the bird into pieces and pour the sauce over it. Reheat in a slow oven for a few minutes, then serve at once.
Serves 4

GAME TERRINE GLENFARCLAS

This is one of the recipes which my cousin George Grant sent me. You will see that he is quite specific about the spirit of the recipe.

1 large pheasant, about
  1.5 kg/3 lb
120 ml/4 fl oz/½ cup
  sweet vermouth
120 ml/4 fl oz/½ cup
  Glenfarclas malt
  whisky

a dozen or so black
  peppercorns, or a
  mixture of black,
  white and green
  peppercorns

2 cloves of garlic,
  crushed
250 g/8 oz/½ lb streaky
  bacon, rind removed
  and finely chopped

3 or 4 pickled walnuts,
  chopped
1 bay leaf

Take the pheasant meat off the bone, and chop it into large bite-sized pieces. Prepare a marinade with the vermouth, whisky, peppercorns and garlic. Marinate the bird for 24 hours.

Preheat the oven to 180°C/350°F/gas 4.

Line a loaf tin with a thin layer of chopped bacon and put in half the pheasant, then more bacon. Lay the walnuts along the middle, cover them with bacon, and add the rest of the pheasant. Cover this with the last of the bacon and a bay leaf. Cover it with baking foil and bake the terrine for 1¾ hours.

Let it cool, turn it out, chill and slice. Serve it with hot buttered toast, and perhaps a crisp salad based on chicory and watercress.
Serves 4

PHEASANT WITH GIN AND JUNIPER

Gin is flavoured with juniper. I have also successfully substituted an *eaux-de-vie*
such as Poire William and Mirabelle in this receipe.

In King Harold's records,
prior to the Norman
Conquest, the pheasant
was listed as a royal bird.
Knights would take 'the
Oath of the Pheasant', a
ceremonial pledge to
some act of honour.

*2 pheasants, each about
1 kg/2 lb*
*90 g/3 oz fat belly of
pork or unsmoked
bacon fat*

*120 g/4 oz/¼ lb streaky
bacon*
120 g/4 oz/½ cup butter
salt and pepper
*6 juniper berries, lightly
crushed*

100 ml/3½ fl oz gin
*175 g/6 oz/½ cup
redcurrant or rowan
jelly*
2 oranges, or 1 if large

*cayenne pepper or
Tabasco sauce*
1 teaspoon dry mustard

Preheat the oven to 250°C/475°F/gas 9.

Lard the birds with pork or bacon fat and truss
them. Line the bottom of the roasting pan with
strips of bacon, add the butter and sprinkle with
pepper. Rub each bird with salt and pepper, and
put 3 juniper berries inside each. Roast them in
the oven for 15 minutes, then pour the gin over
them. Turn the oven down to 180°C/350°F/gas 4
and continue to cook for another 30 minutes or

so, basting from time to time.

Meanwhile, make the sauce. Melt the redcurrant jelly in a pan, add the grated rind of 1
orange, some cayenne pepper or Tabasco sauce,
mustard and the juice of both oranges.

Serve the pheasants on a hot dish with the
cooking juices strained over them, and hand the
sauce separately.
Serves 6

FAZAN PO KAVKAZKI
CAUCASIAN PHEASANT

This is a recipe from Georgia, in the south of the Soviet Union. I prefer to cook
the dish in easy stages, preparing the walnuts the day before I need them. They are
very fiddly, but worth the effort, because the taste and texture when you have
bothered to skin them makes all the difference to the dish. I like lots of walnuts in
this. Guinea fowl adapts well in lieu of pheasant.

*1 large pheasant, about
   1.5 kg/3 lb
250 g/8 oz/1⅓ cups
   shelled walnuts
milk to cover*

*120 g/4 oz/½ cup butter
750 g/1½ lb/5 cups
   muscat grapes, peeled
   and pipped
120 ml/4 fl oz/½ cup*

*strong green tea
(Lapsang will do or
Gunpowder,
preferably, if green
tea is not available.)*

*120 ml/4 fl oz/½ cup
   sweet muscat wine
4 blood oranges
salt and black pepper*

Put the walnuts in a saucepan and cover generously with milk. Bring this to the boil, simmer
for 1 minute, then leave it to cool. Strain off the
milk (use it to flavour some other recipe). Peel
the skin off the walnuts. This reminds me of
brain surgery because of the shape of the nuts
and the difficulty of persuading the skin out of
the curves and crevices. I have been known to
use tweezers to facilitate this. Preheat the oven to
230°C/450°F/gas 8.

Brown the bird quickly but thoroughly all
over in the butter. Reserve one-third of the
grapes for adding just before serving. Coarsely
chop the remaining grapes, and put the bird,
walnuts, grapes, tea, wine and grated rind and
juice of 1½ blood oranges into a casserole. Slice

the remaining oranges thinly. Lay these overlapping on the breast of the bird and on the top of
the surrounding mixture. Season, and pour on
the melted butter in which you browned the
bird. Cover tightly and roast in the oven for 15
minutes.

Lower the heat to 180-190°C/350-375°F/gas
4-5. Leave 20 minutes, then check to see how the
birds are doing. Baste them with the juices, and
if the bird needs a little more time cover and
complete the cooking.

Remove the bird and nuts with a slotted
spoon, and keep warm. Reduce the cooking
liquid if necessary, adjust the seasoning, and add
the reserved grapes. Serve with steamed rice.
Serves 4

PHEASANT WITH STILTON OR ROQUEFORT

This is Nicola Fletcher's recipe. I have sometimes changed it by adding nutmeg to the white sauce, or by leaving the white sauce out altogether and cooking the bird on a bed of chopped leeks to which I have added butter and a little stock. A last-minute dash of cream and nutmeg makes it even better.

King Henry VIII was very partial to pheasant on his feast menus, and he employed a French priest (why a priest?) whose sole concern was the care and fattening of the pheasants.

1 large pheasant, about 1.5 kg/3 lb
175 g/6 oz/¾ cup

Stilton or Roquefort 250 g/8 oz/½ lb leeks
salt and black pepper

75 g/2½ oz/5 tablespoons butter
1 rounded tablespoon

flour
300 ml/10 fl oz/1¼ cups milk

Crumble a quarter of the cheese. Very gently slide your finger under the skin of the pheasant, reaching as far as possible over the breast and legs as well. Push the cheese under the skin in a smooth layer over the flesh. Preheat the oven to 180°C/350°F/gas 4.

Wash the leeks and trim them. Stuff the green tops inside the birds to give flavour and moisture. Season.

Melt 30 g/1 oz/2 tablespoons butter in a small ovenproof dish that will hold the pheasant snugly and put the bird upside down in the dish. Roast it in the oven for 30 to 40 minutes. During the cooking turn the bird on to each of its sides,

basting frequently. When it is done, turn the oven right down, set the bird the right way up, baste again, and leave it in the oven to rest while you prepare the sauce.

Slice the remaining leeks finely and soften them in the rest of the butter in a pan with the lid on. Do not let them brown. Scatter flour on top to absorb the butter and beat the liquid to remove any lumps. Stir in the milk bit by bit, and simmer gently for 10 to 15 minutes. Purée the sauce. Return it to the pan and crumble in the remaining cheese. Season and serve with the pheasant.
Serves 4

PHEASANT AMARETTO

The Italian liqueur Amaretto is made from apricot kernels. Little Hunza apricots, easily found in health food shops, taste sublime soaked in Amaretto. Keep their stones as you eat them, let them dry and crack them open for their kernels. It is worth the effort. Here is a recipe for pheasant or guinea fowl, using an Amaretto and Hunza mixture.

1 pheasant or guinea fowl, about 1 kg/2 lb
salt and black pepper
4 rashers of streaky bacon

60 g/2 oz/¼ cup butter
6 tablespoons gin
150 ml/5 fl oz/⅔ cup double cream

12 or so Hunza apricots, soaked overnight in Amaretto

toasted chopped apricot kernels (preferable) or almonds, to garnish

Hold the bird quickly under boiling water, rub it with salt and pepper, and then tie the bacon slices over the breast. Cook it with the butter, in a pan with a lid, over a low heat for 40 to 45 minutes or until tender. I prefer to cook the bird on its side. Turn and baste it once or twice.

Remove the pheasant from the pan, and flambé with the gin. Warm the spoon first; this makes it easier. Cut the bird up and arrange it on a dish. Keep this warm.

Heat up the cooking liquid, but not right to boiling point, then slowly add the cream a little at a time, stirring. This way, it should not curdle. Season.

Meanwhile, heat up the apricots in their soaking liquor. Arrange the hot fruit round the pheasant pieces, add some of the Amaretto to the cream sauce, to taste, and then pour this over the bird. Sprinkle with the chopped kernels or nuts.
Serves 3

GROUSE

The Glorious Twelfth is the name given by hunters to the day in August when the grouse shooting season begins in Britain. Teams of paid beaters move ahead of the hunters, thrashing the bushes and heather to startle the birds which then rise into the air to be bagged by the guns.

The flesh of grouse is dark and delicious, with a distinctive taste, due to its diet of heather shoots and wild berries. Black grouse, or black-cock, is the size of a pheasant, but the more familiar bird is the smaller red grouse. In the United States, the British grouse is the bird known to Americans as willow ptarmigan and British ptarmigan is what the Americans call rock ptarmigan. Other species of grouse include the dusky grouse in Mexico and the southern states, blue grouse in the northern states and Rocky Mountain areas, ruffed grouse, and both the prairie chicken and sage cock are also grouse.

Obviously the sizes of each species vary, but a rough guide is one grouse per person as a desirable quantity to offer guests. To find out the age of grouse, in order to decide how best to cook them, test the beak and skull. An old bird has a firm beak and hard skull, and may be tough if roasted, in which case use a casserole-type recipe, soup, terrine or pie. A young bird has a more pliable beak and fragile skull, and will roast well. Pheasant recipes can be used for grouse.

ORIENTAL GROUSE

2 grouse, about 1 kg/ 2 lb each
250 g/8 oz/1⅓ cups hazelnuts
500 g/1 lb/3 cups
muscat grapes
3 blood oranges
100 ml/3½ fl oz/⅓ cup Madeira or muscat wine
100 ml/3½ fl oz/⅓ cup strong green tea (Lapsang will do if green tea is not available)
1 tablespoon butter
salt and black pepper
grated nutmeg
60 ml/2 fl oz/¼ cup sour cream or yoghurt

Marinate the grouse overnight, breasts down, in the 'general' marinade mixture given on page 15.

Preheat the oven to 230°C/450°F/gas 8 and roast the grouse briefly, basting. Remove them while it is still rather rare; this will take about 30 minutes. Cut it into portions and put these into a flameproof casserole.

Rub the nuts to remove as much of the skin as possible, then pound them. Crush and sieve the grapes, peel and slice the oranges, and put both in the casserole with the grouse meat.

Make a sauce with the nuts, wine, tea, butter and seasonings. Heat this to boiling point, add the sour cream or yoghurt, mix, pour over the portions of bird, cover and keep just below boiling until the grouse finishes cooking. Serve hot.
Serves 4-6

COLD GROUSE TERRINE

5-6 grouse (any age or condition)
500 g/1 lb lean pork
60 g/2 oz belly of pork
1 medium onion
3 small black truffles
salt and whole black peppercorns
bay leaves
dash Worcestershire sauce
500 g/1 lb streaky bacon, thinly cut
1¾ l/3 pints/7½ cups stock made with
grouse carcasses and/or chicken bones and/or cracked veal knuckle

Use only the breasts of the grouse for this dish; use the rest for stock, or for mincing into another recipe. Remove all tough fibres and skin from the breasts and cut them into pieces. Lay each piece between two layers of greaseproof paper and beat it flat.

Mince together the lean and fatty pork, and add the finely chopped onion and coarsely chopped truffles, salt, peppercorns, bay leaves and Worcestershire sauce. Preheat the oven to 160°C/325°F/gas 3.

Line a flameproof pie dish with overlapping rashers of bacon. Spread the grouse fillets with minced pork and truffle and onion mixture, and lay one on top of the other. Cover with rashers of bacon and pour in some of the stock until it comes halfway up the filling. Cover the dish with foil and a lid and stand it in a roasting tin with water to come halfway up the sides. Cook in the oven for 2 hours. Top up the roasting tin with boiling water if necessary.

While the terrine is cooking, reduce the remaining stock by boiling rapidly, and when the pie is ready fill it up with this. When the pie has cooled, put a sheet of greaseproof paper on top and some weights. When quite cold, remove these and scrape off the fat which will have risen to the top of the pie. Serve sliced with a crisp green salad and baked potatoes.
Serves 8

BLACK ANGUS GROUSE

The black Angus cattle of Aberdeenshire are prime beef. They also supply a
delicious heavy cream when used for milking which provided the original
inspiration for this recipe.

*4 grouse, about 1 kg/
2 lb each, halved
flour, seasoned with salt
and black pepper*

*120 g/4 oz/½ cup butter
4 shallots, chopped
250 g/8 oz/3½ cups
sliced mushrooms
(ideally chanterelles)*

*500 ml/16 fl oz/2 cups
sour cream, at room
temperature*

*1 heaped teaspoon
rowan jelly
120 ml/4 fl oz/½ cup
stock
1 teaspoon dried thyme*

Roll the grouse halves in seasoned flour, then
sauté in the butter.

Remove the grouse pieces and sauté the shallots and mushrooms in the same dish. Return the
grouse to the dish and add the sour cream,
rowan jelly and stock. Sprinkle with thyme,
cover and cook in the oven for about 1 hour.
Serves 8-10

NORWEGIAN CAPERCAILLIE WITH SOUR CREAM AND CHEESE

*1 capercaillie, about
4 kg/8 lb
120 g/4 oz/½ cup butter*

*300 ml/10 fl oz/1¼ cups
sour cream
600 ml/1 pint/2½ cups*

*stock
4 rashers of bacon
120 g/4 oz/¼ lb gjefost*

*(brown Norwegian
goat cheese), grated
salt and black pepper*

Melt the butter in a casserole and brown the bird
all over in this. Add the sour cream and stock
and simmer gently for about 3 hours, until the
bird is tender. Meanwhile, grill the bacon till
crisp and crumble it.

Take the bird out of the cooking liquid and
keep it warm. Thicken the sauce with grated
Norwegian cheese and season it to taste. Carve
the capercaillie and pour the sauce over the
pieces of bird. Sprinkle the crumbled bacon over
the top, and serve.
Serves 8

SWEDISH POT ROASTED CAPERCAILLIE

The capercaillie is the largest member of the grouse family and weighs an average of 4 kg/8 lb or 2–2.5 kg/4–5 lb plucked and drawn. Unlike most birds it should be drawn as soon as it is shot, then it should be hung for a week or longer. If possible, when the bird is drawn reserve and trim its liver, then freeze until needed.

1 capercaillie, about 4 kg/8 lb
about 1 kg/2 lb potatoes, peeled and cut into large chunks
salt and black pepper

1–2 broad, thin rashers of fatty bacon
2–3 tablespoons butter
300 ml/10 fl oz/1¼ cups stock

SAUCE:
300 ml/10 fl oz/1¼ cups juices from the roast, made up with extra stock if necessary

3 tablespoons plain flour
300 ml/10 fl oz/1¼ cups double cream
3 tablespoons redcurrant or rowan jelly

Draw the capercaillie with raw potatoes for several hours, then rinse it thoroughly, dry it and rub seasoning inside and out. Truss the bird, and bard it with the fatty bacon. Melt the butter in a casserole and put the bird into this, breast downwards. Brown the bird all over, moisten with hot stock, cover with a tight-fitting lid and let it cook over a gentle heat for 2 hours or longer if necessary. Baste and moisten during cooking.

When the bird is done, remove and keep in a warm place. Skim and strain the juices, adding more stock if necessary. Thicken with flour, mix well and cook until slightly reduced. Add the cream and heat through without boiling. Add the jelly, let it melt and mix it in well. Check the seasoning. Carve the bird and serve the sauce separately.
Serves 8

The capercaillie, or cock o' the woods, is very fond of feeding on the tips of young pine trees. This gives the flesh a resinous flavour, which can be removed by stuffing the bird with peeled raw potatoes for a few hours before cooking, then removing them before the bird is cooked. The potatoes have the effect of drawing the flavour out and absorbing it, so throw them away afterwards.

BLACKCOCK WITH RED CABBAGE

The blackcock or black grouse has a very handsome tail display, which is sometimes seen on a Scots bonnet. The female, much smaller, is called a greyhen. It is a handsome and tasty grouse, almost twice as large as the common red variety. In France it is known as *coq de bruyère*. The bird is distributed over the highlands of north and central Europe, and central and northern Asia, and a closely similar species is found in the Caucasus. It should be hung for at least a week; otherwise it tends to be dry and rather tasteless. It can be cooked the same way as pheasant and partridge, and the best dishes are those with a good sauce or juice, for example a tasty casserole.

1 blackcock, about 1.5 kg/3 lb, or 2 greyhens, about 1 kg//2 lb each
1 medium red cabbage, finely sliced
2 or 3 apples, peeled, cored and sliced
1 large onion, finely chopped
1 tablespoon brown sugar
whole allspice berries and cloves
150 ml/5 fl oz/²/3 cup dry red wine
250 ml/8 fl oz/1 cup water
salt and black pepper
3 tablespoons wine vinegar
100 g/3½ oz/7 tablespoons butter
1.2 l/2 pints/5 cups stock
2 tablespoons wine vinegar
juice and grated zest of 1 lemon
2 sticks of celery, chopped
2 bay leaves

Mix the cabbage, apples, onion, sugar, spices, wine and water in a saucepan. Season, and let this come just to the boil. Immediately lower the heat, add 3 tablespoons vinegar and cook very gently for about 3 hours, turning from time to time.

Meanwhile, melt 2 tablespoons of the butter in a heavy casserole, and lightly brown the birds. Add the stock, vinegar, lemon zest and juice, chopped celery and bay leaves. Let this simmer very gently for about 1½ hours, then remove the birds and celery. Reserve the celery and discard the bay leaves.

When the cabbage is cooked put the birds on top without a lid, and let them heat through thoroughly. Heat up the celery with the rest of the butter, and serve it with the blackcock and red cabbage.
Serves 4-6

SCANDINAVIAN POT ROASTED PTARMIGAN

*2 ptarmigans, about
  1.1 kg/2¼ lb
salt and black pepper
2 rashers of streaky
  bacon or belly of pork*

*for barding
2 tablespoons butter
300 ml/10 fl oz/1¼
  cups stock, or slightly
  more*

*SAUCE:
300 ml/10 fl oz/1¼
  cups juices from
  cooking, made up
  with stock*

*2 tablespoons plain flour
ptarmigan livers
2 tablespoons redcurrant
  or rowan jelly
175 ml/6 fl oz/¾ cup
  double cream*

Clean, wash and dry the birds thoroughly, re-serving the livers for the sauce. Then rub season-ing into the skins, and sprinkle more inside. Truss and bard the birds. If using the oven, pre-heat this to 160°C/325°F/gas 3. Melt the butter in a casserole and put them into this, breasts down-wards. Sear well. Moisten with hot stock, and cover with tight-fitting lid. Cook in the oven or over a gentle heat for about 1 hour. Baste several times during the cooking. Meanwhile, trim and chop the livers.

When the birds are cooked and tender, lift them out of the pan and keep them warm. Skim and strain the cooking liquid. Deglaze the pan with some of the liquid and sprinkle with a little flour, which you should then mix thoroughly with the pan residue. Mix in the rest of the cook-ing liquid and stock. Sieve the livers and add these.

Cook the sauce for about 5 minutes, then add the jelly and let this melt into the mixture. Add the cream, bring the heat back to just below boil-ing and adjust the seasoning. Carve the birds, pour a little sauce over the pieces and serve the rest separately.
Serves 4

My kilt pin, when I was little, was a grouse claw mounted in silver. The grouse family have feathered legs. I used to look admiringly at ptarmigan pins, with soft, rather fluffy white feathers. Mine seemed rather subdued and drab next to these flashy fellows, and when they were topped with a local cairngorm or amethyst – well, I was sure it would have made all the difference to my sword dance or Highland fling if I had sported one of those.

PARTRIDGE

The name of the partridge derives from the Greek *perdix*, via Latin and French. Perdix was the name of a woman in Greek myth, or possibly of her son. He was thrown from a rampart of Athene's temple by his uncle Daedalus. Athene turned the youth into a partridge as he rushed through the air. There was a sanctuary in honour of Perdix the partridge (or mother of the partridge) beside Athene's temple on the Acropolis.

An interesting point is that one of Athene's names was Onkē, meaning a pear tree. Could this shed a glimmer of light on the old Christmas carol?

Male priests of Athene used to perform dances in imitation of the mating dance of the male partridge as it seeks to impress the hen. The mating call of a cock partridge attracts rival partridges so quickly that hunters used to cage a cock as a decoy to lure others to the area.

PARTRIDGE IN A PEAR TREE PIE

4 small partridges (or one large pheasant), about 1.5 kg/3 lb in all	30 g/1 oz/2 tablespoons pine kernels	firm, peeled, cored and sliced	salt and black pepper grated nutmeg
60 g/2 oz/¼ cup butter	120 g/4 oz/¼ lb spinach leaves	1 ½ tablespoons brandy	500 g/1 lb puff pastry
	2 large pears, ripe but	175 ml/6 fl oz/¾ cup double cream	2 egg yolks
			60 ml/2 fl oz/¼ cup single cream

Remove the flesh from the birds. The carcasses and bones will make a good stock.

Melt half the butter and gently brown the pieces of bird. Remove them and lightly fry the pine kernels in the same pan. Reserve these. Wash, blanch, drain and refresh the spinach leaves. Drain them again and chop. Melt the remaining butter and add the pears and 1 tablespoon brandy. Bring to boiling point, then remove the pieces of pear. Add the spinach, bird, pine kernels and cream. Season and add grated nutmeg. Preheat the oven to 230°C/450°F/gas 8.

Put a layer of pear slices on the bottom of a buttered pie dish, then spread on the partridge and spinach mixture, and top with the remaining pears. Cover with pastry and bake in the oven for 20 minutes.

Ease the pie crust up and pour in a mixture of egg yolks beaten with cream and the rest of the brandy. Replace the lid and let it cook for 5 more minutes. Serve piping hot.
Serves 4

SPANISH PARTRIDGES WITH CHOCOLATE

This sauce tasts nothing like a chocolate pudding. One ingredient is a catalyst for another, and the resultant sauce cannot be recognized as chocolate flavoured. In an anticipatory fit of chocoholism, I broke off a piece of Hershey's unsweetened chocolate which I had brought back from America in order to test the recipes using chocolate. It was like taking a mouthful of plain flour. I spat it out in disgust. Without the addition of sugar, and maybe vanilla, and even milk, raw chocolate bears no relation to the familiar addictive substance. If you are unable to get unsweetened chocolate, use the most bitter cooking chocolate you can find. It will still work. Adjust the other seasonings to taste, but remember, this is not chocolate as our tastebuds know and love it.

4 small partridges, less
   than 500 g/1 lb each
salt and black pepper
30 ml/1 fl oz/2
   tablespoons brandy
flour to dredge
4 tablespoons oil or lard

1 onion, chopped
1 green pepper, chopped
4 cloves of garlic,
   chopped
2 tablespoons chopped
   fresh parsley
2 bay leaves

1 teaspoon thyme
¼ teaspoon ground
   cinnamon
1 large, tasty tomato,
   peeled
250 ml/8 fl oz/1 cup
   water or stock

1 teaspoon salt
1 tablespoon vinegar
50 g/1¾ oz/1¾ squares
   unsweetened dark
   bitter chocolate,
   grated

Clean the partridges and rub them inside and out with salt and pepper and brandy. Let them sit for 30 minutes, then dredge them in flour and brown them slowly in the hot oil or lard. When they are browned, add the chopped onion, pepper and garlic. Fry a few minutes more, then add the parsley, bay leaves, thyme, cinnamon, whole peeled tomato and water or stock. Add the salt and vinegar. Cover, and simmer until the birds are tender, about 20 minutes.

Remove them to a serving dish. Pass the sauce through a sieve and return it to the pan. Add the grated chocolate and cook very slowly until it is melted, adding more stock as needed to make a smooth sauce. Pour over the partridges.

I sometimes add some green chilli, chopped very finely (make sure you never include any seeds – instant dragon's breath!) to the herb and vegetable mixture.
Serves 4

Don't be put off by the idea of meat with chocolate. The use of chocolate in game and poultry dishes goes back to South and Central America before the Spanish conquest, and the Mexican national dish *mole* is a surviving recipe of that type. Indeed, in ancient America chocolate was considered too special and important to be squandered on women or slaves, and was reserved for high dignitaries and their lesser men. Go to it, sisters!

RUSSIAN PARTRIDGES IN CREAM AND RAISINS

*2 partridges, about
    750 g/1½ lb each
salt and black pepper
1 tablespoon flour*

*4-5 tablespoons butter
1 tablespoon cognac
60 ml/2 fl oz/¼ cup
    stock or strong*

*consommé
90 ml/3 fl oz/⅓ cup
    single cream or sour
    cream*

*2 tablespoons raisins or
    blackcurrants
175 g/6 oz/6 slices
    white bread, cubed*

Cut the birds in half, and flatten by beating between two sheets of greaseproof paper. Rub salt and pepper into them, cover in flour, and sauté them quickly in 2-3 tablespoons butter. Put them in a casserole, pour cognac over, cover with a lid and bring to a low boil. After 1 minute add the stock, cream and raisins or blackcurrants, and cook, covered, over a very low heat for 10 minutes. Meanwhile, fry the bread in the rest of the butter to make croûtons, and use these to garnish the birds.
Serves 4

SPANISH PICKLED PARTRIDGES

Herodotus reports that a popular food in ancient Egypt was small birds, some of them pickled in brine for a few days and eaten without further preparation. This Spanish reecipe is probably very similar, except that it uses sweet peppers, which did not arrive in the Old World until the beginning of the sixteenth century.

*6 small partridges, less
    than 500 g/1 lb each
salt
900 ml/1½ pints/3¾
    cups dry white wine
500 ml/16 fl oz/2 cups*

*vinegar
250 ml/8 fl oz/1 cup
    olive oil
2 tablespoons capers
1 teaspoon black
    peppercorns*

*10 whole cloves
4 sweet red peppers, cut
    into strips
1 chilli pepper, seeds
    removed, finely
    chopped*

*4 bay leaves
2 whole heads of garlic,
    peeled
1 veal marrow bone*

Simmer all the ingredients over a low heat for 2 hours, or until the birds are tender. Meanwhile sterilize some screw-topped, wide-mouthed preserving jars.

Let the birds cool and put them into jars. Discard the marrow bone, pour the liquid over the partridges and seal. Store in a cold larder or fridge. You may strain the liquid or keep the spices in the mixture, according to taste. I think it looks prettier with some of the peppers and spices in the jars.
Serves 6

PARTRIDGES MORISCO

1.5 kg/3 lb breasts and
 thighs (partridges,
 guinea fowl, or any
 other)
1½ lemons
salt and black pepper
8 globe artichokes
120 g/4 oz/½ cup butter

250 ml/8 fl oz/1 cup
 olive oil
2 tomatoes, peeled,
 seeded and roughly
 chopped
60 g/2 oz/1 cup
 parsley, chopped

1 tablespoon crushed
 fresh ginger
½ teaspoon ground
 cumin
½ teaspoon saffron
1 stick of cinnamon
500 ml/16 fl oz/2 cups
 stock

good handful of stoned
 green olives
1 egg, beaten
fresh toasted
 breadcrumbs to coat
pinch of cayenne pepper

Sprinkle the birds with juice of half a lemon, salt and pepper, and put in a cool place until needed.

Wash and trim the artichokes, then boil them in salted water containing 2 tablespoons of lemon juice. When they are tender, drain them and let them cool, then remove the leaves and chokes. Scrape the flesh off the bottoms of the leaves and blend it to a purée; reserve bottoms.

Sauté the birds in a casserole with a mixture of butter and olive oil until the pieces are lightly coloured. Transfer 3 tablespoons of this cooking fat to another pan and reserve. Add to the birds the tomatoes, parsley, 1 teaspoon of lemon zest and the ginger, cumin, saffron and cinnamon. Pour on the stock, and simmer for 30 minutes or until tender. Just before you finish cooking, add the olives.

Dip the reserved artichoke bottoms into beaten egg and coat them with breadcrumbs. Sauté them in the reserved oil until golden, and serve them with the puréed artichoke flesh and the partridges. Sprinkle with a little cayenne pepper before serving.
Serves 6

RAJASTHANI STUFFED PARTRIDGE OR QUAIL

2 partridges or 4 quail
STUFFING:
1 tablespoon oil
2 onions, chopped
1 green chilli
*2 cloves of garlic,
  crushed*

*1 teaspoon ginger paste,
  or 2.5 cm/1 in fresh
  ginger root, crushed*
*½ teaspoon grated
  coriander*
*½ teaspoon chilli
  powder*

*250 g/8 oz/½ lb lean
  minced meat, lamb or
  beef*
*a few fresh coriander or
  mint leaves*
2 teaspoons lemon juice
grated zest of ½ lemon

1 teaspoon garam masala
1 large fresh tomato
*12 almonds, blanched
  and chopped*
*90 g/3 oz/½ cup
  seedless raisins*
salt and pepper

Bone the birds, or have them boned for you if possible.

Heat the oil in a heavy-based frying pan. Reserve 2 teaspoons of chopped onion and blanch this in boiling water to add later. Fry the rest until soft and golden. Finely chop the green chilli, being very careful to remove every seed: if you leave any, your guests' mouths will be set on fire. Add the chilli with the crushed garlic and ginger to the pan. In a small bowl, mix the coriander and chilli powder with a little cold water, then add this to the pan and continue to cook for 5 more minutes, stirring frequently so that nothing sticks. Add the minced meat and stir again. Leave the mixture to cook over a very low heat until the moisture is absorbed.

Chop the coriander or mint leaves finely and stir these into the stuffing, together with lemon juice and zest, garam masala, chopped tomato, so that the consistency is thick and fairly dry. Add the blanched almonds, remaining onions and raisins at this point. Add salt and pepper to taste. If using the oven, preheat it to 180°C/350°F/gas 4.

Stuff the birds with this mixture, and use fine skewers to close them up, or else stitch them with a large eyed needle and fine string. They may be cooked in oil in a wok, or in the oven either in a roasting tin or individually wrapped in foil. Partridges will take about 30 minutes in a roasting tin, 35 minutes in foil; quail 20 minutes in the tin or 25 minutes in foil.
Serves 4

INDIAN PARTRIDGE WITH CREAM SAUCE

3 partridges, about
   500 g/1 lb each
5 onions
1 heaped teaspoon
   ground cinnamon
500 g/1 lb stewing veal,
   including bone
2.5 cm/1 in fresh
   ginger, thinly sliced

or chopped
1 teaspoon salt
90 g/2 tablespoons
   coriander seeds,
   lightly crushed
75 g/3 oz/6 tablespoons
   ghee (clarified butter)
2 cloves
2 bay leaves

5 cloves garlic, crushed
   in a little water
a generous pinch of
   grated nutmeg
juice of 1 fresh lime
   (preferably) or ½
   lemon
¼ teaspoon saffron

175 g/6 oz/1½ cups
   ground blanched
   almonds
175 ml/6 fl oz/¾ cup
   double cream (or
   thick yoghurt)
4 cardamoms, lightly
   crushed

Clean and dry the partridges. Crush 4 onions to a paste with the ground cinnamon, and coat the partridges with this. Leave them for 30 minutes, then scrape the mixture off into a pan, and wipe the birds with absorbent kitchen paper. Refrigerate the birds.

Prepare a stock with the veal, the chopped onion mixture, ginger, salt and crushed coriander. Simmer for about 2 hours, until the liquid has reduced to about 450 ml/15 fl oz/2 cups. Strain and reserve it. Heat 30 g/1 oz/2 tablespoons ghee with the cloves and bay leaves, and when this is hot, and the flavours have infused into the fat, add the stock. Cover and leave for a few minutes over low heat.

Heat the rest of the ghee with the remaining onion, finely chopped, and most of the crushed garlic, reserving 1 teaspoon of this. When the onions have turned colour, add the partridges; cover and place on low heat, occasionally giving the pan a shake, until the partridges have browned slightly. Preheat the oven to 160°C/325°F/gas 3.

Uncover, add the nutmeg and 300 ml/10 fl oz/1¼ cups of the stock, cover and simmer for a further 45 minutes or so, until no moisture remains and the birds are tender. Moisten with the lime juice and remaining teaspoon of garlic. Flavour the remaining stock with saffron. Mix the almonds with double cream and cardamoms. Add the stock, pour the mixture over the cooked partridges, adjust the seasoning, cover with a tight-fitting lid, shake, and cook in the oven for 20 minutes.

Serves 4-6

PERSIAN RICE WITH BITTER CHERRIES AND PARTRIDGES

Shiraz in Persia is known as the city of the roses: its city gates are covered with a frieze of rose-blazoned tiles. But my disappointment was bitter when I went to visit the tomb of the poet Hafiz, and it was explained to me that the city's progressive mayor had felt that such a poet deserved a 'worthy' monument, and so had had the city build something modern. Ceramic roses again, but mercifully the old tomb with its glorious ancient tiles was still there, tucked away behind the glitter.

The roses of the desert around Shiraz were surely the Quashqai tribeswomen. Dressed in brilliant lurex and tinsel, and at that time unveiled, they herded their dusty black goats near the ruins of Persepolis. The souk of Shiraz is filled with vivid giant roses on everything, bolts of gaudy, gauzy fabrics cascading over carpets and copper, pyramids of fruit and sacks of spice. In that city I ate a dish of steamed rice cooked with bitter cherries and served with plump partridges, a meal which ended with the perfumed muskmelons of the region.

This rice dish is also a delicious accompaniment to a shoulder of venison, and extra sour cherries may be served on the side, with a dish of thick yoghurt.

4 partridges (or 6-8 quail) about 1.5 kg/ 3 lb in all	60 g/2 oz/heaped ⅓cup sugar	about 250 ml/8 fl oz/ 1 cup stock or water	juice of ½ lemon ¼ teaspoon saffron threads, pounded in a
1 kg/2 lb fresh, ripe bitter cherries, stoned	3 tablespoons olive oil salt 1 medium onion, chopped	60 g/2 oz/ ¼ cup butter 425 g/14 oz/2⅓ cups basmati rice, washed and soaked	pestle and mortar and soaked in a little warm water

Clean, split and flatten the birds.

Put the cherries and sugar into a medium-sized saucepan, and bring to the boil over a high heat, stirring gently. Reduce the heat and simmer, uncovered, until the cherries have softened a little and the juices have run out. Remove the pan from heat.

Heat the olive oil in a large, heavy casserole. Pat the birds dry and sprinkle them inside and out with salt. Brown the birds in the hot oil, turning frequently so that they cook without burning. Remove them and set aside in a bowl so that no juice is lost. Add the onion to the oil. When this has browned nicely, return the birds and all of the juices to the casserole, add some stock or water, bring to the boil, then cover and reduce the heat. Simmer for about 30 minutes, or until they are tender.

Meanwhile, melt the butter in a large, heavy pan; add the drained and rinsed rice, and stir well. Add the lemon juice and mix well again. Pour water to a level 2 cm/almost 1 inch above the rice, stir and bring to the boil, then lower the heat and simmer. Cover with a close-fitting lid and continue to simmer until the water has been absorbed by the rice or the rice is cooked.

Add the cooking liquid from the birds to the rice, stir and bring back to a simmer. Then take a few tablespoons of rice and mix this in a separate bowl with the dissolved saffron, until the rice is bright yellow. Mix the cherries into the remaining rice, quickly, so that you keep clarity in the mixed colours. Heat, uncovered, for a few minutes, then arrange the cherry rice and birds on the large serving platter, using the saffron rice as decoration sprinkled on top.
Serves 4 to 6

SPANISH PARTRIDGES WITH GARLIC

1.5 kg/3 lb total weight of partridges (or pigeons or quails)
juice of ½ lemon
2 tablespoons flour
salt and black pepper
120 ml/4 fl oz/½ cup olive oil
1 large onion, chopped
250 ml/8 fl oz/1 cup dry sherry
about 1.75 l/3 pints/7½ cups stock
60 g/2 oz/1 cup parsley, chopped
2 dried hot red peppers,
or ½ teaspoon crushed dried hot red pepper
1 bay leaf, crushed
120 g/4 oz/⅔ cup blanched slivered almonds
2 tablespoons butter
4 large cloves of garlic,
thinly sliced
1 teaspoon ground cumin
5 egg yolks, lightly beaten
stoned green olives, to garnish

Cut the birds into pieces. Pour the lemon juice over the birds and sprinkle them with seasoned flour. Sauté them in olive oil until they are lightly coloured. Remove them from the pan and set aside.

Sauté the onion until translucent. Add the sherry and simmer the mixture until it is reduced to a glaze, about 60 ml/2 fl oz/¼ cup. Return the birds to the pan and add enough stock to almost cover them. Add most of the parsley, the peppers and the bay leaf, cover with buttered paper and simmer until tender. Transfer the birds to a warm platter and strain the stock. Sauté the blanched slivered almonds in the butter until they colour. Add the sliced garlic and sauté until golden.

Mix in 500 ml/16 fl oz/2 cups stock, the cumin and salt and pepper to taste. Remove from heat and stir in the lightly beaten egg yolks. Cook over very low heat, stirring so that the eggs don't scramble or curdle. Mask the birds with this sauce, and garnish with stoned olives and the remaining parsley.
Serves 4

TITAR KE SULE
PARTRIDGES COOKED ON A SKEWER

This can also be made under a grill. It is important to keep basting the birds to ensure that they are moist.

4 partridges
30 g/1 oz/2 tablespoons ghee (clarified butter)
8 cloves of garlic
1 tablespoon of lemon juice
MARINADE:

4 green cardamoms
4 cloves
8 black peppercorns
2.5 cm/2 in/ stick of cinnamon
2 large onions, chopped, puréed to

make a paste, lightly fried
500 ml/16 fl oz/2 cups thick yoghurt
1 teaspoon red chilli powder
salt

FOR DHUNGAR
(SMOKING):
charcoal pastilles (from church supplies shops, or perhaps a Greek supermarket)
3 cloves
a few drops of ghee

Bone the partridges, or have them boned for you. Beat them flat, then cut them in halves.

Prepare the marinade. Grind the whole spices, or pound them in with a pestle and mortar. Mix all the marinade ingredients together, coat the partridge pieces in this and leave them to absorb the marinade for at least 4 hours.

Take a little metal bowl which will hold the burning charcoal, and place this in the centre of a large pan which has a tight fitting lid. Arrange the marinated partridge pieces around the little bowl, light the charcoal, lightly crush the cloves and sprinkle them on the glowing embers, then sprinkle a few drops of ghee to make it smoke fragrantly. Quickly cover with the lid, and let the smoke infuse the partridges.

Crush the cloves of garlic with a little water. This will be used for basting the birds.

Skewer the partridge pieces, about 2.5 cm/1 in/1 in apart, and grill them over the lowest possible heat for 30-40 minutes. A charcoal grill is best. Baste the birds alternately with ghee and the garlic water.

Serves 4

QUAIL

Wild quail are migratory birds, and in the autumn in California and the American southwest the hunters eagerly await their arrival. They fly in bevies of about a hundred. But because of their tender flesh, they have long been raised for the table. The Lisle Letters, written during the sixteenth century, recount that baskets of cheeping quail were sent backwards and forwards between houses as gifts, and were accepted with the same delighted response with which today's hostess accepts flowers or chocolates. In the film *Babette's Feast*, a dish of quail, *Cailles en sarcophages*, is crucial to the unfolding of this tender story, and our mouths water as Babette prepares her surprise.

Recently, smoked quail and smoked quail eggs have appeared in our shops, adding further range to the versatility of this little bird.

Most quail are bought from shops ready plucked and cleaned. Their flesh is delicate and, unless they are to be stuffed, it is best to leave them whole. When stuffed, they should be boned first – a task which is almost unbearably fiddly, but worth the effort. Never skin quail; the skin helps to retain the moisture and flavour. One stuffed quail per head makes a reasonable portion, but if they are whole and unstuffed you must allow two.

Quail on toast harks back to medieval times when food was served on a trencher or slab of bread which served as a plate. This sopped up the juices, and at the end of the meal was thrown to the underlings.

QUAILS *LA TRAVIATA*

Perhaps this dish could be offered on the supper menu at Covent Garden.

8 quails
a little butter
salt and black pepper

300 ml/10 fl oz/1¼ cups champagne
150 ml/5 fl oz/⅔ cup

good jellied veal stock, made previously with a

split veal knuckle

Put a steamer on to boil. Butter greaseproof paper. Season the birds and wrap each one in a piece of paper. Steam them over high heat for 15 minutes.

Preheat the oven to 180°C/350°F/gas 4. Let the quail rest for 10 minutes, then transfer them to a ovenproof dish, unwrap them, and pour in the champagne. Finish cooking them in the oven, covered, basting frequently with champagne. Remove them from the dish, keep them warm, and prepare a glaze, using the juices and champagne, and jellied veal stock. Reduce over heat, adjust seasonings, and pour over the birds. Serve them hot, or cold set in the jellied champagne glaze.

Serves 4

Quail, roe deer and girls, when in a group, are all known as a bevy.

MOULD OF QUAILS ANTIQUARIO

For some years, during the great Florence Biennale, the art and antiques fair, magnificent banquets were prepared, based on historical feasts and ancient recipes. Guiseppe Bellini was one of the main inspirational forces behind these occasions, and I am indebted to him for sending me the following recipe inspired by the ancient Etruscans.

12 quails
marinade made from oil,
  red wine, sage, salt
  and black pepper

100 g/3½ oz/7
  tablespoons butter
3 tablespoons flour
500 ml/16 fl oz/2 cups

milk
4 eggs, lightly beaten
2 slices of prosciutto,
  with fat, minced

25 g/¾ oz truffles
100 g/3½ oz/1¾ cups
  fresh breadcrumbs

Marinate the quails for several hours.

Take the meat off the bones and mince this finely. Make a béchamel sauce with 60 g/2 oz/¼ cup of the butter, the flour and milk, then add the beaten eggs, the minced prosciutto and quail, and 15 g/½ oz grated truffles. Preheat the oven to 180°C/350°F/gas 4.

Use the rest of the butter to grease a mould, and line this with breadcrumbs. Pour in the mixture. Stand the pan in a roasting tin of boiling water and cook in the oven for 1 hour, or until the mould comes away from the sides of the dish.

Turn out the mould and serve with the remaining truffles arranged in thin slices on top.
Serves 6

RUSSIAN CHERRY QUAILS

8 quails
250 g/8 oz/½ lb fresh
  sour cherries, stoned

60 ml/2 fl oz/¼ cup
  stock

1 tablespoon cognac
100 g/3½ oz/7
  tablespoons butter

salt and black pepper

Preheat the oven to 230°C/450°F/gas 8. Fry the quails gently for 3 to 5 minutes in a flameproof casserole, turning. Then pour off the fat, add the cherries, stock and cognac, and roast, uncovered, for 10 minutes. Season with salt and pepper.
Serves 4

QUAILS WRAPPED IN VINE LEAVES

8 quails
60 ml/2 fl oz/¼ cup oil
  or butter, plus more
  butter for frying bread

1.2 cm/½ in fresh
  ginger, peeled and
  slivered
juice of 1 lemon and a

little zest
ground cinnamon
salt and black pepper
vine leaves to wrap

8 slices of fatty pork
500 ml/16 fl oz/2 cups
  stock
8 slices of crustless bread

Brown the quails quickly in oil or butter. Put a few little slivers of ginger and a strip of lemon zest inside each bird, sprinkle with lemon juice, a little ground cinnamon, salt and pepper, then wrap each one in vine leaves. Tie a piece of fatty pork over the top of these little parcels, then sim-

mer them gently in stock in a covered casserole for about 40 minutes.

Meanwhile, fry the slices of bread. Remove the quail parcels, unwrap, and serve, each one a slice of fried bread.

Serves 4 to 6

QUAILS WITH GRAPES

8 quails
6 tablespoons butter
500 g/1 lb/3 cups grapes

250 ml/8 fl oz/1 cup
  grape juice
about 120 ml/4 fl oz/½

cup stock
30 ml/1 fl oz/
  2 tablespoons cognac

salt and black pepper

Preheat the oven to 230°C/450°F/gas 8. Fry the quails in 2 tablespoons of butter in a deep pan for 5 minutes. Add the grapes, the rest of the butter and the grape juice. Add stock as required and

simmer gently for 25 minutes. Transfer to a roasting pan, sprinkle with cognac and roast in the oven for 10 minutes. Season.

Serves 4

QUAILS STUFFED WITH OYSTERS

4 quails
fresh oysters, 1 or 2 per
    bird will usually do

175 g/6 oz/¾ cup
    butter
salt and black pepper

4 thin slices of lemon
4 broad, thin rashers of
    fatty bacon

100 ml/3½ fl oz/⅓ cup
    champagne

Preheat the oven to 230°C/450°F/gas 8. Stuff each bird with oysters, a little butter, salt, pepper and a thin slice of lemon. Bard the birds with bacon and roast them with the rest of the butter for 20 minutes. Remove the barding fat, return the birds to the oven to brown, basting well with pan juices. Remove the birds, pour off excess fat, and deglaze the pan with the champagne. Adjust seasonings and serve.
Serves 4

SMOKED QUAILS WITH *KASHA*

4 smoked quails
1 onion, chopped
2 bay leaves
120 g/4 oz/1 cup celery,
    diced (optional)
120 g/4 oz/heaped 1

cup carrots, diced
    (optional)
175 g/6 oz/scant 1 cup
    kasha (buckwheat),
    washed
1 tablespoon olive oil

120 g/4 oz/1⅔ cups
    mushrooms, (or, if
    you can get them,
    chanterelles), sliced
120 g/4 oz/heaped ¾
    cup broad beans,

podded
3 or 4 spring onions,
    chopped
a little grated lemon zest
salt and black pepper

Take the flesh off the quails, dice the meat and set it aside. Simmer the bones with chopped onion and bay leaves in about 600 ml/1 pint/2½ cups water for 30 minutes. You may add diced celery and carrot to this stock, if you like.

Heat the olive oil, and sauté the sliced mushrooms gently. Add the buckwheat, then pour in the stock from the simmered bones. You may add the stock vegetables, but not the bones. Add the broad beans. Simmer for 15 minutes or so until the liquid is absorbed.

Add the quail flesh, chopped spring onions, lemon zest and salt and pepper to taste. Serve this with a dish of soured cream, or soured cream and horseradish.
Serves 4

SMOKED QUAIL GRATIN

This is delicious made with either ordinary or sweet potatoes, and the tart addition
of rhubarb is surprisingly good. Perhaps not, after all, so surprising!

6 smoked quails
6 medium-sized potatoes
* or sweet potatoes*
1 clove of garlic
30 g/1 oz/2 tablespoons

butter
salt and black pepper
freshly grated nutmeg
pinch of ground
* cinnamon*

3 sticks of rhubarb,
* chopped*
¼ teaspoon fresh ginger,
* very finely chopped*
dash of sweet wine

(optional)
300 ml/10 fl oz/1 ¼
* cups Jersey milk*
375 ml/12 fl oz/1 ½
* cups double cream*

Preheat the oven to 180°C/350°F/gas 4. Peel and
wash the potatoes or sweet potatoes, pat them
dry and slice them as thinly as possible.

Rub an ovenproof earthenware dish with the
peeled garlic (chop the end a little, so that the
juices run when you press it against the sides of
the dish), and dot it generously with most of the
butter. Make a layer of potatoes and season it
with salt, pepper, nutmeg and cinnamon. Make
a layer with the rhubarb and season with crushed
ginger, cinnamon and pepper. Put the quails on
top, evenly spaced, then another layer of
potatoes, and season again. Continue making
layers of potatoes, seasoning each layer. Add a
dash of sweet wine if you like. Combine the
milk and cream, and pour it over the dish. Dot
the top with the remaining butter and bake for
about 2 hours. Serve very hot.
Serves 3-4

PIGEONS AND SQUABS

In Britain we tend to think of pigeons as pests. They eat the farmers' crops, and town dwellers consider them dirty and a nuisance. But in Mediterranean and Arab countries, pigeon and squab are considered delicacies, and they are still raised in special towers, just as the Greeks and Romans used to do. In fact, this was once the case in Britain, where pigeons used to be an important part of winter's diet and most villages, farms and manor houses had dovecotes, many of which have survived.

Pigeons are available all the year round. Squabs are young pigeons 4 to 6 weeks old; they are specially reared and fattened, and their flesh is lighter in colour than the meat of wood pigeons, which tends to be dry. Squab is very tender and easily damaged, and requires gentle handling.

In some restaurants it is currently fashionable to serve just the breast of pigeons, perhaps as a warm salad or in an exotically flavoured sauce.

STRATHSPEY PIGEONS

4 plump pigeons, about 750 g/1½ lb each
salt and black pepper
30 g/1 oz/2 tablespoons butter
1 tablespoon olive oil

1 large onion, chopped finely
175 g/6 oz/2½ cups field mushrooms (or chanterelles, if you can get these), chopped

3 tablespoons Glenfarclas malt whisky
150 ml/5 fl oz/⅔ cup dry white wine
150 ml/5 fl oz/⅔ cup stock

1 tablespoon lemon juice
good pinch of cayenne pepper
4 tablespoons double cream
chopped parsley for garnish

Divide each pigeon in half and remove the backbone, using a sharp little knife and poultry shears or good kitchen scissors. Season well with salt and pepper. Heat the butter and oil together in a pan and brown the pigeons thoroughly. Remove them and keep warm.

Fry the onions until they are soft, then add the mushrooms. When all of these are cooked, return the birds to the pan. Pour on the warmed whisky and set this alight. When it has stopped flaming add the wine, stock, lemon juice and cayenne, and bring the mixture to a brisk simmer. Cover and reduce the heat to a very gently simmer and cook until tender, which may take as little as 30 minutes or as much as 2 hours, depending on the pigeons. You may need to add more stock.

Adjust the seasoning. Just before serving, stir in the cream and sprinkle with parsley.
Serves 6

NOUNOU'S NEW YEAR PIGEONS WITH OLIVES

I spent New Year some years ago with friends in Greece. They were keen
sportsmen and had returned from shooting in the Thessalonika region. The
pigeons were quickly plucked and prepared for the following dish. Use olives
which have been preserved in oil, not brine.

*4 small wild pigeons or
squabs, about 500 g/
1 lb each
fatty bacon for larding
1 large onion, chopped*

*90 ml/3 fl oz/7
tablespoons good
olive oil
6 large potatoes, peeled
and thickly sliced*

*175 g/6 oz/1 ¼ cups
black olives, unstoned
dried thyme, preferably
still on twigs
grated zest of 1 lemon*

*salt and black pepper
about 300 ml/10 fl oz/1
¼ cups stock made
with wine*

Clean the pigeons and lard them with the bacon.
Soften the onion in about 1 dessertspoon of olive
oil. Lightly brown the pigeons.

In a separate casserole, arrange the sliced
potatoes to make a bed for the pigeons. Add the
onion, smoothing it over the potatoes. Scatter
over the olives, and put in the pigeons. If you
have sprigs of thyme, lay these under and between the pigeons; otherwise sprinkle the dish
generously with dried thyme. Sprinkle on the
lemon zest and seasonings. Dribble the rest of
the olive oil over the dish, add most of the stock,

and cover.

Cook over a low heat until the pigeons are
tender. With wild birds this may need 1 ½ to 2
hours, but squabs will take half that time. When
you test, you may want to add more stock.
Serve with crusty bread and a lusty red wine.

You can, if you like, make a sauce by taking
some of the cooking liquid and some of the extra
stock, heating, adjusting the seasoning (perhaps
add a little fresh lemon juice) and mixing in some
good thick Greek yoghurt at the last moment.
Serves 4

SQUABS CORTEZ

This dish, named after the conquistador, follows the practice which the Spanish brought back from America – using a little chocolate in the sauce. If this alarms you, reassure yourself by reading the introduction note on page 33.

The Romans raised thrushes for the table, feeding them millet, crushed figs and wheat flour. They fed snails on milk until they were too fat to squeeze back into their shells. Dormice were considered a great delicacy and fattened on nuts. An unpleasant Roman habit was to break the legs of squabs and clip their wings, to ensure the minimum of mobility and the maximum of tender flesh.

4 squabs, about 500 g/
  1 lb each
75 g/2½ oz/5
  tablespoons butter
salt and black pepper

4 slivers of lemon zest
2 tablespoons olive oil
4 large, mild Spanish
  onions, chopped

2 cloves of garlic
300 ml/10 fl oz/1¼
  cups dry white wine
150 ml/5 fl oz/⅔cup
  stock

15 g/½ oz/½ square
  unsweetened chocolate
1 tablespoon cornflour
1 teaspoon fresh lemon
  juice

Wipe the birds inside and out and rub them with about 15 g/½ oz/1 tablespoon of the butter seasoned with salt and pepper. Put the slivers of lemon zest inside each bird. Melt 30 g/1 oz/2 tablespoons of butter and quickly brown the birds all over. Set them aside.

Add the oil to the pan and gently cook the chopped onions and garlic until transparent. Return the squab to the pan, add the wine and stock, bring to boiling point, then lower the heat and simmer until they are tender (about 50 minutes). Remove the birds and keep these hot. Boil the stock to reduce it, remove it from the heat, and stir in the chocolate. Mix the remaining 30 g/1 oz/2 tablespoons butter thoroughly with the cornflour to make a *beurre manié* and stir this into the sauce until it thickens smoothly. Add a little lemon juice, taste, season, return the birds to the sauce, heat through and serve.
Serves 4

BISTELA
MOROCCAN PIGEON PIE WITH ALMONDS

8 small pigeons, about 500 g/1 lb each
500 g/1 lb/2 cups butter
3 soup bowls full to the brim with chopped parsley
1.5 kg/3 lb/8 cups onions, chopped finely or grated
2 teaspoons salt, or to taste
1 teaspoon black pepper
½ teaspoon saffron
2 teaspoons ground cinnamon
200 g/7 oz/1 cup sugar
600 ml/1 pint/2½ cups water
8 eggs, beaten
300 g/11 oz/scant 2 cups blanched almonds
40 ml/1⅓ fl oz/2⅔ tablespoons oil
500 g/1 lb filo pastry
a little icing sugar

Wash the pigeons and put them whole in a thick-bottomed saucepan. Add 300 g/10 oz/1¼ cups of the butter, the parsley, onions, salt, pepper, saffron, ½ teaspoon of cinnamon and the sugar, and water. Cover and cook on medium heat, stirring from time to time, until the pigeons are tender, about 1½ hours.

Take the pigeons out of the saucepan and remove any flavourings that may have got inside them during cooking. Reduce the cooking liquid, adjust seasonings, and remove from heat. Add the beaten eggs, and pour over, gently stirring all the time, so that it becomes creamy. Cut up the pigeons without boning. Fry the almonds in the oil until they begin to colour, then turn out at once into a strainer retaining the oil. Crush them coarsely in a mortar or pass through a vegetable sieve, using the coarsest grid. Add to the filling. Also add 2 tablespoons of the oil in which the almonds have been fried, and reserve the remainder of the oil.

Preheat the oven to 180°C/350°F/gas 4. Melt the rest of the butter in a small pan and add the remaining oil. Brush a little of this over the inside of a very large, shallow ovenproof dish.

Line the dish with about one-third of the sheets of filo pastry, overlapping them and leaving the ends hanging over the edge of the dish. After each sheet is laid in place, brush it all over with a little melted butter and oil.

Spread half the pigeon and filling in the dish and lay about one-third of the remaining filo sheets over it, brushing with butter and oil as before. Spread on the rest of the pigeon and filling. Top with the last of the filo sheets, again brushing each out with butter and oil after it is laid in place. Turn all the projecting ends of the sheets in over the top of the pastry to make a decorative rim.

Bake the *bistela* for about 45 minutes, then turn the oven up to 200°C/400°F/gas 6 and bake for a further 15 minutes to brown the top. Before serving, sprinkle the crust with the rest of the cinnamon mixed with a little icing sugar.
Serves 12

BISTELA 2

This version is smaller and slightly less aggressively exotic – but still excitingly
unusual in its blend of flavours. Instead of squabs, you could use wood pigeons.
First marinate these in a red wine marinade, then simmer them in this. Strain this
cooking liquid and use it as the moistening agent. The resulting pie will be
delicious, but gamier.

3 squabs, about 500 g/
  1 lb each
1 large onion, finely
  chopped
120-175 g/4-6 oz/2-3
  cups parsley, chopped
½ tablespoon chopped

fresh chervil
½ teaspoon saffron
½ teaspoon ground
  ginger
1 tablespoon ground
  cinnamon
1 teaspoon lemon juice

salt and black pepper
175 g/6 oz/¾ cup
  butter
300 ml/10 fl oz/1¼
  cups water
175 g/6 oz/1 cup
  blanched almonds

90 g/3 oz/¾ cup icing
  sugar
8 eggs
250 g/8 oz/½ lb filo
  pastry

Put the birds in a large pan with the onion, half
the parsley, the chervil, saffron, ginger, half the
cinnamon, lemon juice, salt and pepper. Add
half the butter and some little water, season,
cover the pan and cook gently. Let them simmer
for about 50 minutes. Add water as required, to
produce a flavoursome sauce. Meanwhile,
lightly brown the almonds in a little more butter, then crush and mix them with most of the
icing sugar, reserving about 1 tablespoon.

Beat the eggs with the remaining parsley.
Strain the cooking liquid from squabs and add as
much of this to the eggs as will be necessary to
give a good, moist pie filling. Adjust the seasonings. Heat this egg mixture to the consistency of
soft scrambled eggs. Pull the squabs to pieces,
discard the bones and skin, and mix the pieces of
flesh into the mixture.

Preheat the oven to 180°C/350°F/gas 4. Put
several layers of filo pastry over the sides and
base of an ovenproof dish, brushing with melted
butter between each layer, and allowing the
pastry to fall over the sides of the dish. Spread a
layer of almond mixture over them, then a layer
of filo, then a layer of the egg and squab mixture.
Moisten with some of the cooking liquid, then
cover with more layers of buttered filo. Continue until you have used up the fillings in suc-
cessive layers as above, finishing with layers of
buttered filo. Turn the edges in to make a frilled
border and bake in the oven until browned,
about 1 hour. Sprinkle with the remaining icing
sugar mixed with cinnamon before serving.
Serves 4-6

TRID
MOROCCAN PANCAKES STUFFED WITH PIGEON

These are made with *rghaif* dough, a simple unleavened mixture of flour and water. They are traditionally cooked on the rounded upper surface of a large earthenware pot with a hole at each end, known as a *qdra dial trid*. It is propped in place on stones and filled with embers to heat it. You could improvise with a wok set upside-down over a barbecue, or simply use an ordinary dry griddle. The filling for the pancakes can be made with chicken or lamb instead of pigeons. You could substitute filo pastry for the rghaif dough.

pigeons, chicken, or lamb, to give about 750 g/1½ lb meat after preparation, cut into about 20 pieces

salt
1 teaspoon black pepper
good pinch of saffron
1 teaspoon ground ginger
1 stick cinnamon

1 tablespoon chervil, chopped
1 tablespoon parsley, chopped
3 large onions, chopped
120 ml/4 fl oz/½ cup

water
200 ml/7 fl oz/scant 1 cup olive oil
500 g/1 lb/heaped 3 cups flour

Gently simmer the meat, salt and pepper, spices and herbs, onions, water and half the olive oil, in a heavy casserole with a tight-fitting lid.

Make a simple dough with the flour and very little water, adding a spoonful from time to time. Work it thoroughly, then make it into balls about the size of small hens' eggs. You will have enough dough to make about 20 of these. Lightly oil aboard, and flatten each of these dough balls into a very thin disc, about 20 cm/8 in across. Cook each of these on your *qdra dial*

trid (or improvised alternative). It must not be too hot, and each side of each pastry disc must be cooked. Arrange half of these cooked pancakes in an ovenproof dish, overlapping each other and coming up the sides of the dish. When the meat is tender, remove the cinnamon stick, and arrange the meat on top of the pancakes. Cover with the remaining pancakes, tucking the edges in. Pour a little of the cooking liquid over the *trid*, and serve the rest separately as a sauce.
Makes about 20 pancakes: Serves 6

In his *Moorish Recipes*, John, fourth Marquis of Bute, suggests that this dish might well have been introduced into Morocco in the time of Mulai Idris, descendant of the Prophet Mohammed, who fled to Morocco from Mecca, and whose body lies buried at Fez, the land of his exile. It is reputed to be the oldest Arab dish, and it is said that when the Prophet Mohammed was asked what he liked best in the world, he answered that he loved his wife above everything, but after her he loved *trid*.

SALMI DI PALOMBE
UMBRIAN JUGGED WOOD PIGEONS

March and October are the right months for shooting pigeons in Umbria. Their diet has been acorns and berries, which impart a special flavour to the flesh. If your pigeons have been shot under similar conditions, be it in Italy or anywhere else, try this recipe.

*2 large pigeons, each
  1 kg/2 lb
100 ml/3½ fl oz/⅓
  cup green extra-
  virgin olive oil
1 medium onion,
  chopped*

*1 medium carrot,
  chopped
1 stick celery, chopped
1 tablespoon chopped
  parsley
sprig of sage, or 1
  teaspoon dried sage*

*sprig of thyme, or 1
  teaspoon dried thyme
4 cloves
100 ml/3½ fl oz/3⅓
  cup dry red wine
120 ml/4 fl oz/½ cup
  vinegar*

*salt and black pepper
1 anchovy, chopped
1 clover of garlic,
  crushed
4 large slices of bread*

Clean and wash the birds. Cut them into pieces and fry in the olive oil with the chopped onion, carrot, celery and parsley for a few minutes. Add the sage, thyme, cloves, wine and most of the vinegar, reserving 1 tablespoon, and season with salt and black pepper. Cook over a low heat for about 1 hour, simmering gently but not boiling.

Strain the gravy, then mix it with the chopped anchovy, crushed garlic and remaining vinegar. Heat this sauce, pour it over the pigeons and serve them hot with toasted or fried bread.
Serves 4

PALOMBACCI ALL'USO D'AMELIA
PIGEONS AS COOKED BY AMELIA

*2 large pigeons, about
  750 g/1½ lb each
500 ml/16 fl oz/2 cups*

*dry red wine
zest of ½ lemon,
  finely sliced*

*3 or 4 cloves
salt and 5 or 6 black
  peppercorns*

2 cloves of garlic

Pluck and wash the pigeons. Draw them, reserving the heart, the liver and the outside of the crop. Replace these inside. Cook on a spit for about 10 minutes without any seasoning, to allow them to send out all the moisture in their not-very-moist flesh. (If you do not have a spit, roast them in a hot oven, 220°C/425°F/gas 7, turning several times.) Combine the other ingredients in a bowl.

Brush the birds with oil after the first 10 minutes' cooking. Then allow them to continue cooking slowly for more than 1 hour (if using an oven, turn it down to 160°C/325°F/gas 3). Baste the birds frequently with the liquid mixture so they do not dry out.

When they are cooked, remove the entrails and chop these while you keep the birds warm. Strain the cooking liquid and mix in the chopped entrails. Cut the birds into pieces and arrange them on a serving dish. Pour the liquid mixture over them as a sauce.

Serves 4

PICCIONI IN SALVIA ALL'USO DI FOLIGNO
PIGEONS WITH SAGE IN THE MANNER OF FOLIGNO

This Italian regional speciality has its own peculiarity. You must not remove the pigeons' entrails, only the crop. According to gourmets, this is what gives the dish its characteristic flavour.

2 large pigeons, each 1 kg/2 lb
2 medium onions, chopped
4 or 5 cloves
½ lemon, or more to taste, thinly sliced
handful of sage leaves
30 g/1 oz/2 tablespoons chopped ham
50 ml/1¾ fl oz/2⅓ tablespoons olive oil
50 ml/1¾ fl oz/2⅓ tablespoons vinegar
salt and black pepper

Pluck and wash the pigeons and remove the crops. Put them in a flameproof earthenware pot with the chopped onions, cloves, sliced lemon, sage, chopped ham, olive oil, vinegar, salt and black pepper. Cover the pot and leave it all to simmer gently over a low heat for about 1 hour, or until the flesh begins to come away from the bones.

Serves 4

An Australian recipe goes like this: 'Take a pigeon, and a stone the same size. Place both in the oven. When the stone is tender, so is the pigeon.'

PICCIONI COL RISO
PIGEONS WITH RICE

Pigeons are very underrated in Britain, which is a pity, because they are easily
available in most big supermarkets, and although they are small they are also
inexpensive and very tasty. Try this simple and rather comforting dish on a cold
winter's evening. Any leftovers can be made into a delicious soup.

*2 large pigeons, about
    750 g/1½ lb each
salt and black pepper
2 sprigs of fresh sage*

*4 tablespoons oil
120 g/4 oz/¼ lb ham
    with fat
1 large onion, chopped*

*1 tablespoon tomato
    purée
250 g/8 oz/1⅓ cups
    Italian arborio rice*

*60 g/2 oz/½ cup grated
    Parmesan cheese*

Clean the pigeons, reserving the livers, and
singe them over a flame. Put salt, pepper and
fresh sage inside. Put the pigeons in a pan with
half the oil and the chopped fat and lean ham.
Cover the pan with the lid, stretching kitchen
towel under the lid to absorb the moisture.
Leave to cook over a low flame, removing the lid
only to turn the birds, until they are tender – 50
minutes to 2 hours depending on the birds.

Meanwhile, wash and drain the rice. In a
separate pan, lightly fry the chopped onion in
the rest of the oil. When just coloured, add the
chopped livers and tomato purée. Cook briefly,
stirring, so that the livers don't become tough,
then add the rice. Cover the pan and let the rice
absorb the sauce as it cooks, adding stock from
time to time as required. When the rice is tender
– about 20 minutes – season it with salt, pepper
and grated Parmesan, and serve it, authentically,
first on its own, then with the pigeons cut in
halves (or if you prefer, all together).
Serves 4

PHOENIX PIE

Named for Phoenix, Arizona. Phoenix the bird might not be game, but wild
turkey certainly is. Failing wild turkey, use domestic.
This pie is definitely a relation to the Moroccan *bistela* (pages 49 and 50), via
European medieval pies that were later taken to North America by the
conquistadores – I have adapted it from a recipe in Huntly Dent's *The Feast of
Santa Fe: Cooking of the American Southwest* (Simon & Schuster, 1985).

500 g/1 lb/3 ½ cups
   cooked turkey breast,
   chopped
60 g/2 oz/ ⅓ cup
   blanched, slivered
   almonds
2 tablespoons icing
   sugar
1 teaspoon ground
   cinnamon

½ medium onion,
   chopped
2 cloves of garlic, finely
   chopped
3 tablespoons butter
½ teaspoon ground
   allspice
½ teaspoon ground
   ginger

½ teaspoon turmeric
¼ teaspoon ground
   cloves
60 ml/2 fl oz/¼ cup
   Madeira or sweet
   white vermouth
1 tablespoon lemon juice
3 eggs plus 1 yolk
60 g/2 oz/1 cup

chopped parsley
3 tablespoons raisins
1 teaspoon grated orange
   zest
salt and black pepper
shortcrust pastry made
   with 250 g/8 oz/1½
   cups flour and 120 g/
   4 oz/½ cup fat

Roast or grill the almonds gently until they turn brown. Allow them to cool a little, then grind them coarsely in a blender and combine with the sugar and half the cinnamon. Blend for a few more seconds, and set aside.

Combine the onion and garlic in a pan with the butter and cook gently until transparent. Add the spices and stir over medium heat for 1 minute. Add the turkey meat, Madeira and lemon juice, and bring to the boil. Beat 3 eggs with the parsley in a small bowl, and add all at once to the pan. Cook these until the eggs become soft curds. Remove from the heat, and add the raisins, orange zest, and salt and pepper to traste. Line a pie dish with chilled pastry. Spread a layer of sugared almonds on the bottom, then the turkey mixture. Top with another thin layer of pastry, decorate, and chill until ready to cook, then preheat the oven to 220° C/425° F/gas 7.

Brush the crust with beaten egg yolk, then bake the pie for 30 minutes. Sprinkle the top with icing sugar and cinnamon before serving.
Serves 4

CHINESE PIGEON PARCELS

A variation on the familiar theme of wrapping a meaty filling in an edible leaf: vine
leaves, cabbage leaves, blackcurrant leaves, all make good wrappers. I think the
crispness of lettuce enhances this dish.

*2 large pigeons or 4
    squabs, about
    1.5 kg/3 lb in all
6 tablespoons oil
1 medium onion,
    roughly chopped
2 stalks of celery, diced*

*6 water chestnuts (may
    be tinned), diced
4 beanshoots (may be
    tinned), sliced
6 large mushrooms,
    sliced (or, if you can
    get them, oyster*

*mushrooms,
    shredded)
1 teaspoon shredded
    fresh ginger
3 tablespoons light soy
    sauce
2 tablespoons medium
    sherry*

*120 ml/4 fl oz/ ½ cup
    stock
about 1 tablespoon
    honey, or to taste
1 tablespoon cornflour
4 large leaves from an
    iceberg or Webb
    lettuce*

Take the flesh off the pigeons and cut it into
rough cubes. Heat 3 tablespoons of oil and sauté
the pigeon meat for 10 minutes.

Take it out of the pan, add the rest of the oil
and when this is hot quickly sauté the vegetables
and the ginger – but not the lettuce – for a few
seconds. Then add the soy sauce, sherry and
stock. Add honey cautiously, testing as you add
it. Let the whole thing simmer for a few seconds
while you mix the cornflour to a paste with a
little cold water. Stir this in, add the pigeon,
bring back to the boil and cook for 30 seconds.

Put a spoonful of this mixture in the centre of a
crisp Webb or iceberg leaf, roll it up and skewer
with a wooden toothpick. Serve at once.
Serves 4

GUINEA FOWL

One year my mother reared guinea fowl in the orchard, instead of geese. They were very decorative, but much too tempting a prospect for raider foxes to resist. In France, guinea fowl are given a spoonful of cognac before killing, to improve the flavour rather than from any intention to anaesthetise, although it probably does both jobs well enough. Our guinea fowl had to do without, as indeed we had to do without the guinea fowl.

The Greeks and Romans liked to include these 'hens of Numidia' in banquets, but then their popularity faded, except in France. Then in about 1530 the Portuguese started to import guinea fowl to Europe again, bringing them from West Africa. Although they are not strictly gamebirds in the same sense as pheasants and grouse, guinea fowl can be interchanged with pheasant in any recipes, so I have included it, as I have included quail, which is generally reared, not shot. Both quail and guinea fowl do exist in the wild, as well as being reared under free-range conditions.

The legs of guinea fowl can be rather dry and stringy, but the rest of the flesh is delicious.

SPICED SALMIS OF GUINEA FOWL WITH CORIANDER AND CUMIN

2 guinea fowl, each about 1 kg/2 lb
4 rashers of streaky bacon
1 Valencia or blood orange, quartered
60 g/2 oz/¼ cup butter
1 onion, finely chopped
1 tablespoon ground coriander
2 teaspoons ground cumin
600 ml/1 pint/2½ cups stock
juice and grated zest of 1 lemon
1 teaspoon capers, drained
salt and black pepper

Preheat the oven to 220°C/425°F/gas 7. Bard the breasts of the birds with bacon, securing these with string or cotton. Put the orange pieces inside each bird. Brown the birds quickly in a pan with 30 g/1 oz/2 tablespoons butter, then roast them in the oven for 30 minutes, basting frequently. Remove from the pan and set aside.

When the birds have cooled slightly, discard the skin, then remove all the meat from the carcass and chop this roughly. Add the remaining butter to the juices in the roasting tin, and fry the onion in this. Let it become transparent but not brown. Stir in the coriander and cumin, and cook, stirring, for a few minutes. Add the stock and bring it to the boil. Transfer the mixture to a large saucepan, add the carcasses, cover and simmer for 30 minutes.

Strain the mixture, add the lemon juice and zest, then boil rapidly until the liquid has reduced to about 450 ml/15 fl oz/scant 2 cups. Stir in the capers, and season to taste with salt and pepper. Arrange the guinea fowl pieces in a flameproof dish. Pour the sauce over these and simmer gently for 15 to 20 minutes, or until the meat is tender. Serve at once.

Serves 4

This recipe and the recipe for Peking Duck on page 74 come from Marilyn Aslami's *Harrods Cookery Book* (Ebury Press), to whom I am very grateful for permission to reprint them.

WOODCOCK

The woodcock is a larger cousin of the snipe, and is found almost all over the world. It has a fine delicious flavour. It may be eaten fresh, or hung for a day or so, and it is commonly eaten plucked but undrawn, as the trail, or intestines, is considered a great delicacy.

Woodcock should not be overcooked. It may be grilled lightly, or cooked by any recipe suitable for quail. It is trussed by crossing the legs, bringing its head round and piercing the legs with the beak.

WOODCOCK FLAMBÉ

2 woodcocks, about 1 kg/2 lb each

60 g/2 oz/¼ cup butter 100 ml/3½ fl oz cognac

2 tablespoons dry red wine

1 teaspoon lemon juice salt and black pepper

Preheat the oven to 230°C/450°F/gas 8. Roast the plucked birds in butter for about 15 minutes. Cut them into quarters and keep warm. Chop the intestines finely and mix these with the juices in the roasting dish. Season, pour the cognac over them and set it alight. Reduce the sauce over high heat, then add the red wine, lemon juice, salt and pepper. Cook this for a few moments, then pour over the woodcocks.

Another way of serving the trail is to draw the birds, and cook the trail in butter with basil or marjoram and seasonings. Mash, spread on fried bread, and top with the roasted birds.
Serves 3-4

RICH AND RARE PUDDING

For this recipe you can use any mixture available of game birds (pheasant, partridge, plump pigeon, woodcock, etc.), total weight 1.5 kg/3-4 lb

120 g/4 oz/¼ lb calf's liver
about 150 ml/5 fl oz/ ⅔ cup port
suet crust made with 375 g/12 oz/2½ cups flour and 175 g/ 6 oz/¾ cup suet
250 g/8 oz/½ lb sausage meat
60 g/2 oz/1 cup chopped parsley
2 bay leaves, crushed
750 g/1½ lb stewing beef, chopped
4 juniper berries, crushed
salt and black pepper

Remove the flesh from the birds in large fillets, and marinate it with the calf's liver overnight in the port. Turn it as often as you conveniently can.

Line a large basin with suet paste, not too thickly. Cover this with sausage meat, parsley and crushed bay leaves. Fill with layers of beef and game, and the liver cut in fine slivers. Season with juniper berries, salt and black pepper as you proceed. Pour in the marinade, and cover the pie securely with suet crust which you have rolled out. Cover the basin with a floured cloth and boil it for 8 hours, adding more boiling water as necessary.

Before serving, remove the cloth and brown the top lightly in the oven, then wrap a clean white napkin around the basin.
Serves 10

WATER AND MARSH FOWL

The water-fowl most commonly seen on our tables are various types of duck and geese. The following recipes can be used for wild or domestic fowl. The main difference is in size: a domestic goose has about one and a half times as much meat as a wild one, and you will need to scale up the quantities of the other ingredients. (Of course some wild geese are huge; a Canada goose may weigh more than 4 kg/9 lb. A domestic duck is about twice the weight of a wild mallard and over three times that of a teal. No duck bears a great deal of flesh for its overall size, but what there is is well worth the effort of plucking and cooking. As with any bird, more people can be fed if it is accompanied by a generous stuffing.

Other water- and marsh fowl include the mergansers (fish-eating ducks), swans, rail, coot, crane, woodcock and snipe. The fish-eating birds should be skinned before cooking, because the fish flavours get into the skin and fat and spoils the flavour. (See the instructions on plucking and skinning given on page 155.)

Older birds will benefit from marinating overnight or for 24 hours to tenderize them, after which the meat should be served rare.

A sea bird we do not eat today is the puffin, but in medieval times monks debated the subject of eating puffins on fish days, as the flesh tastes fishy. The opposing argument was that the puffin nests in burrows.

Other monastery debates included the definition of the barnacle goose; fish or fowl? There are some charming illustrations in early manuscripts, which show clusters of shell fish attached to stumps hanging over tide water. When these shell fish ripened, it was said small birds dropped out into the water. These were the young barnacle goslings.

The six-legged goose, on the other hand, did exist, although not in the dramatic shape its name suggests. This refers to the habit of cooking rabbit legs, and pieces of rabbit meat, inside a roasting goose. When the goose was ready, the rabbit meat was permeated with its flavour.

GOOSE

Goose is supposed to be in its prime by Michaelmas (29 September), fattened on the stubble and gleanings left by the reapers. Young rabbits, too, are fat from stolen grain; windfall apples litter the orchard; and onions are ready to be lifted. The conjunction of things such as goose and rabbit in a pie, or roast goose with sage and onion stuffing and apple sauce is no accident, but pre-ordained in the great scheme of things.

ROAST GOOSE WITH ONION, APPLE AND CELERY STUFFING

1 wild goose, about
2.5 kg/5 lb
90 g/3 oz heaped/½ cup
raisins
425 ml/14 fl oz/1¾
cups Madeira

120 g/4 oz/½ cup butter
1 large onion, finely
chopped
1 tart apple, peeled,
cored and chopped
90 g/3 oz/¾ cup celery,

chopped
60 g/2 oz/⅓ cup
pecans, coarsely
chopped
500 g/1 lb/4 cups
toasted bread cubes or

fried croûtons
½ teaspoon sage
salt and black pepper
juice of 1 lemon
1 teaspoon cornflour or
arrowroot

When preparing the goose, reserve the giblets and made stock with them; but save the liver for the stuffing and cut it into cubes. Heat the raisins in a little of the Madeira and let them stand for a few minutes. Pour off any wine that has not been absorbed and reserve it.

Melt 90 g/3 oz/6 tablespoons butter and sauté the onion, apple and cubed goose liver. When the onion is soft, add the celery and mix well. Remove the pan from the heat and add the nuts and raisins. Combine this mixture in a large bowl with the toasted bread cubes or croûtons, sage, and salt and pepper to taste. Let the stuffing cool. Preheat the oven to 200°C/400°F/gas 6.

Sprinkle the cavity of the goose with salt and pepper, pack it loosely with stuffing, and sew up the opening. Truss the bird, spread the skin with the rest of the butter (or you could use rendered goose fat), and sprinkle it with salt. Combine 120 ml/4 fl oz/½ cup Madeira with an equal amount of water and the lemon juice. Roast the goose, breast side up, on a roasting rack for 20 minutes, then reduce the heat to 160°C/325°F/gas 3, turn the bird on its side and baste it with the Madeira mixture. After 30 minutes turn the bird on to its other side, baste again and give it another 30 minutes. Turn it breast side up and continue to roast it, basting it every 10 minutes or so, for another 1½ to 2 hours, depending on the size of the bird. Remove the fat from the pan several times during the roasting, and reserve this for another use.

Transfer the goose to a serving platter, remove the trussing and keep it warm. Pour off any remaining fat from the pan, add another 120 ml/4 fl oz/½ cup Madeira, and deglaze the pan over moderately high heat, stirring in all the bits stuck to the sides of the pan. Add the cornflour or arrowroot, and then some giblet stock, to make a sauce. Simmer for 5 minutes and season to taste. Serve the sauce in a heated sauceboat.
Serves 4

Riddle: What two things grow down?
Answer: Icicles and a goose

OCA AL FORNO
ITALIAN ROAST GOOSE

Allow 750 g/1½ lb undrawn (600 g/1¼ lb drawn) per person.
In ancient Florence roast goose was prepared on All Saints' Day. People who did
not have an oven would use the public oven that stood in a narrow street in the
centre of the ancient city, which is still called *Via delle oche*, 'street of the geese'.

The futility of a wild goose chase is unquestioned. But does this belittle the sport of goose hunting, or is it a tribute to the alertness of all geese? Does it reflect in some way on the watchdogs of ancient Rome, the geese on Capitoline Hill?

1 goose (see note on weight above)
salt and black pepper
4 tablespoons oil

1 large onion, finely chopped
2 medium carrots, finely chopped

2 sticks celery, finely chopped
handful of parsley, finely chopped

100 ml/3½ fl oz/3⅓ cup dry white wine
1 tablespoon butter
2 teaspoons flour

After plucking and drawing the goose remove the neck, singe the bird over a flame, wash and pat it dry. Sprinkle salt and pepper inside and put the bird in a flameproof dish with the oil and onions, carrots, celery and parsley. Preheat the oven to 180°C/350°F/gas 4.

Fry the goose over a high heat, turning to brown it evenly, then cover with greaseproof paper, greased with oil, and a lid. Roast for about 1¼ hours for a 2.5 kg/5 lb wild goose, 1¾ hours for a 5 kg/10 lb tame one, and 20 more minutes for every extra 1 kg/2 lb, 10 minutes for every extra 500 g/1 lb.

When done, put the dish back over a high heat, without a lid, so that the bird gets a golden crust. Remove the bird and keep it warm. Strain the cooking juices, skim off the grease and return the dish to the heat, pouring the dry white wine into it. When the wine has evaporated add the butter well mixed with the flour to thicken the sauce. Adjust the seasoning. Cut up the goose and serve with this sauce in a sauceboat.

SCANDINAVIAN ROAST WILD GOOSE WITH JUNIPER AND GIN

Gin is juniper flavoured, and if it is warmed, then poured over crushed juniper
berries and flambéed, the resultant infusion imparts a most delicious aroma to a
sauce. If you have burnt it too much, and turned the liquid bitter, adjust the taste
with a little sugar and more gin.

1 wild goose, about
  2.5 kg/5 lb
250 g/8 oz/½ lb belly
  of pork, sliced thinly
  (omit if using a
  domestic goose)
750 ml/1¼ pints/3 cups
  chicken stock

4 bay leaves
12 juniper berries,
  lightly crushed
1 tablespoon flour
120 ml/4 fl oz/½ cup
  gin
STUFFING:
6 tablespoons butter

4 onions, chopped
1 stick of celery, diced
3 cloves of garlic, sliced
375 g/12 oz/6 cups
  fresh breadcrumbs
salt and black pepper
1½ tablespoons dried
  sage

½ teaspoon thyme
1 egg, beaten
up to 120 ml/4 fl oz/
  ½ cup stock, or
  water, if needed

Why is there nothing so
irrevocable as cooking
your goose?

Start by preparing the stuffing. Melt the butter
and gently sauté 2 of the onions with the celery
and garlic until the onions are soft. Mix the
breadcrumbs, salt, pepper, sage and thyme in a
bowl, then add the vegetables and butter. Stir in
the beaten egg. The stuffing should be firm, not
wet; but if it seems too dry add some stock or
water.

Salt and pepper the goose inside and out, and
stuff losely. Now either slip the slices of pork
under the breast skin or lay them alongside the
breast. After trussing the legs together, continue
binding with the string to tie the belly of pork
down securely. Preheat the oven to 190°C/
375°F/gas 5.

Put the chicken stock, bay leaves and juniper

berries in a shallow roasting pan. Then put the
goose, breast side up, on a rack in the pan and
roast for about 1 hour (a domestic goose of 4 kg/
8 lb *drawn* weight will take about 1¾ hours).
Baste the bird often with the pan juices, at least 5
or 6 times during cooking.

When the goose is done, remove it from the
pan and keep warm. Skim the excess fat off the
pan, scrape the residue loose, stir in the flour and
make gravy in the ordinary way. Pour in the gin,
quickly set fire to it, blow out the flames after
about 15 seconds and boil the gravy for a few
minutes to reduce it to a good consistency.

Carve and serve the goose with this gravy in a
sauceboat.
Serves 4

ROAST GOOSE WITH APRICOT AND APPLE STUFFING

Edward I gave a Royal Charter to the great Nottingham Goose Fair in 1284. The journey to the goose fair might take days, even a week, and in this case the gooseherd 'shod' his geese. He did this by dipping their feet first into tar, and then into sand. Geese shod in this way are reported to have travelled at the rate of a mile an hour.

1 wild goose, about 2½kg/5 lb
1 teaspoon pickling spices
120 ml/4 fl oz/½ cup dry red wine
250 ml/8 fl oz/1 cup water
1 tablespoon blackstrap molasses
2 apples, peeled, cored and diced
175 g/6 oz/1½ cups dried apricots
100 g/3½ oz/⅔ cup raisins
120 ml/4 fl oz/½ cup lemon juice
salt and black pepper
60 g/2 oz/1 cup fresh breadcrumbs
120 g/4 oz/¼ lb belly of pork, thinly sliced

Prepare the stuffing the night before you plan to roast the goose. Simmer the pickling spices in the wine, water and molasses for 10 minutes or so. Strain, and add the apples, apricots and raisins. Simmer for 5 minutes, cover and leave in a cold larder or refrigerator.

When ready to roast, rub the goose inside and out with lemon juice, then salt and pepper it. Strain the liquid out of the stuffing and reserve this liquid. Stir the breadcrumbs into the fruit. Preheat the oven to 180°C/350°F/gas 4.

Stuff and truss the goose, closing the vent by sewing or skewering. Lay slices of pork over the breast. Place the goose in a rack over a shallow roasting pan and roast it for 2 hours or so, basting frequently with the reserved liquid. Remove the pork before sewing.
Serves 4

CZECH STEWED GOOSE LIVERS WITH ONIONS

1 kg/2 lb goose livers
2 medium onions
60 g/2 oz/¼ cup butter or oil
1 teaspoon caraway seeds
salt and black pepper

Clean the goose livers thoroughly and make a few light cuts on the surfaces. Brown the onions in the fat and add the livers, caraway seeds, salt and pepper. Let them cook gently in their own juices, turning when one side is done. Do not overcook: 5 minutes in all should be enough. Served hot or cold, with fried potatoes.
Serves 4 as a light supper dish

GOOSE CHÂTEAU LE PIN

Many are the delicious feasts I have had at the table of John and Rebecca
Whitehead, both in London and at their Normandy family home, Château Le Pin.
Usually I end the meal feeling more like a Périgord goose than anything else! And
I will never forget being woken by the aggressive blast of a hunting horn outside
my bedroom door. This recipe is just one delicious souvenir.

*1 small domestic goose,
   about 5 kg/10 lb
500 g/1 lb black
   pudding
3 cloves of garlic,
   crushed*

*2 or 3 large dessert
   apples, peeled, cored
   and grated, plus 3
   more to make purée
grated zest of 1 lemon*

*60 ml/2 fl oz/¼ cup
   port
salt and black pepper
30 g/1 oz/2 tablespoons
   sugar, or more to
   taste (but purée*

*should be very little
   sweetened)
60 ml/2 fl oz/¼ cup
   calvados*

When preparing the goose reserve the liver. Skin
the black pudding and pound it smooth with the
liver and garlic. Blend in the grated apples and
lemon zest, and bind the stuffing with port.
Stuff the goose. Prick the skin all over with a
skewer, and rub with salt and pepper.

Preheat the oven to 200°C/400°F/gas 6. Place
the goose in a roasting tin and cover it with foil. I
usually start it roasting breast downwards, then
turn it after half the cooking time. Allow 15
minutes to the 500 g/1 lb. Meanwhile, make

some purée with the remaining apples and the
sugar.

After 1 hour, drain the fat from the pan and
pour 120 ml/4 fl oz/½ cup cold water over the
goose. Remove the foil 30 minutes before cooking is complete, and baste the goose every 10
minutes with the pan juices. Serve the goose on a
thick bed of apple purée, with a good gravy
made with the calvados.
Serves 6

Anatole France describes
the making of a cassoulet
in his *Histoire Comique*:
'Clément's cassoulet has
cooked for twenty years.
He puts into the pot some
goose or fat bacon,
sometimes a sausage or
some more beans, but it
is always the same
cassoulet.' Real cassoulet
is not made, it
accumulates – like the
stockpot which always sat
at the back of the kitchen
range.

KHUBAB HANS
ROAST GOOSE FROM NORTHERN INDIA

1 medium-sized goose
5 tablespoons aniseed,
    crushed
2 tablespoons coriander
    seeds, crushed
250 g/8 oz/½ lb bessan
    (chick pea flour)
a few grains of ground
    sandalwood
    (optional)

STUFFING:
500 kg/1 lb minced meat
4 cm/1½ in fresh ginger,
    finely chopped and
    crushed
2 teaspoons black
    pepper
6 onions, finely chopped
salt
90 g/3 oz/6 tablespoons
    ghee or oil

180 g/6 oz/heaped 1
    cup seedless raisins,
    soaked in a little
    water and lemon
    juice, then chopped
120 g/4 oz/⅔ cup
    blanched almonds,
    toasted
60 g/2 oz/4 tablespoons
    coriander seeds,
    toasted

12-16 cloves garlic,
    finely chopped
4 tablespoons cooked
    basmati rice
1 tablespoon ground
    cinnamon
300 ml/½ pinte/1¼
    cups yoghurt
¼ teaspoon cayenne

Clean and wash the goose thoroughly, pat it dry with absorbent kitchen paper. Fill a large deep pan with boiling water and immerse the goose in this for about a minute. Remove it and prick it all over with a very sharp knife. Rub the aniseed and ground coriander well into the skin. Leave the goose to absorb the spices for a couple of hours, then wash it well, pat it dry and rub the *bessan* into the skin. Mix the sandalwood with a little boiling water, reserve a few drops, and rub the remainder over the goose. Leave it for another couple of hours, then wash it again. This sweetens the goose and gets rid of some of the excess fat.

Meanwhile, prepare a stuffing of the minced meat, ginger, half the black pepper, chopped onions and salt. Brown this gently in a little of the ghee or oil and when it is brown, then the drained chopped raisins and a couple of drops of the sandalwood water. Stuff the goose and truss it well.

Simmer the goose in water until half cooked, about 1½ hours. Preheat the oven to 160°C/325°F/gas 3. Remove it and drain it. Skim any fat from the cooking liquor and reduce it to about 150 ml/¼ pint/⅔ cup. Blend the almonds, roasted coriander, garlic, salt, rice, cinnamon and remaining black pepper. Mix this with the remaining butter and yoghurt, and add the cooking liquor. Roast the goose in the oven, basting frequently with this mixture, for about 1½ hours. Before serving, make a gravy with the residue from the roasting pan, a little water and a dash of cayenne, and serve this with the goose. *Serves 4-6.*

DUCK

Wild duck are an awkward size for formal servings. One is rather more than a portion (fine for a hungry hunter) whereas half is not enough.

When roasting wild duck, it should always be served on the rare side. To over-cook is a sin. It has a special flavour and consistency, different from domestic duck, although the same recipes can be used for either. The exception is if the flesh is fishy or muddy, because the bird has been feeding on sea-shore or mud flats. In such cases, either use a fish recipe (as they do in India, for instance), or skin the bird (see page 155 for a description of how to deal with fish-eating birds such as mergansers), and marinate.

To roast a small duck, I prefer to cook any stuffing separately, and just put herbs, a twist of lemon or orange peel, a small onion studded with a couple of cloves, half a lemon, or some apple slices inside the cavity. A small mandarin orange inside a roasting duck imparts a delicious aroma. I found a description of a dish using small mandarins laid over the bottom of a dish for the final ten minutes of roasting ducks (Dorothy Hartley's *Food in England*, Macdonald (1954). Before serving, the pips were removed, a little butter and sugar added to each fruit, and these, with watercress, made an attractive garnish.

TEAL WITH YOUNG TURNIPS

Teal is a small species of wild duck, beautiful and delicious. In France it is permitted to eat teal on fast and abstinence days. Teal fanatics (I number myself among these) consider that it should be undercooked, in fact 'cooked for no longer than the time it would take to fly through the oven'. Perhaps a slight exaggeration!

2 teal, about 750 g/	*60 ml/2 fl oz/¼ cup*	*young turnips*	*120 ml/4 fl oz/½ cup*
1½ lb each	*sweet white wine*	*salt and black pepper*	*sour cream or strained*
2½ tablespoons paprika	*500 g/1 lb/4 cups diced*	*3 tablespoons butter*	*yoghurt*

Mix 1½ tablespoons of paprika with the wine, and pour it over the turnips in a casserole. Add salt and pepper, and dot with a little of the butter. Cover, and cook gently for 30 minutes. Preheat the oven to 180°C/350°F/gas 4.

Heat the remaining butter in a frying pan and brown the teal. Season. Put the sautéed teal on top of the turnips and roast in the oven for 20 to 30 minutes. When these have cooked, remove the birds from the casserole and keep them warm. Pour off any excess liquid, leaving about 120 ml/4 fl oz/½ cup. Pour the sour cream and the remaining paprika over the turnips, mix them together and heat through without boiling, then lay the teal on top and serve.
Serves 3-4

ROAST CANVASBACK DUCK

The canvasback duck is so called because the colour of its back is much paler than its chestnut-coloured head. It is very fond of eating wild celery shoots, which give its flesh a distinctive flavour. It is very highly thought of in America, and there is a gastronomes' story about a popular New York City restaurant which served this duck. It arrived before the dinner with the duck's head lying along the side of the dish, indicating that it was a canvasback. The legend tells of a single duck whose head made a multitude of appearances.

A simple and tasty way to serve this is to roast it in butter for 25 minutes or so then make a gravy with a glass of red wine and a tablespoonful of redcurrant jelly added to the pan residue, and the sauce reduced until it thickens, then seasoned to taste. Serve this with wild rice.

DUCK WITH ORANGE

Duck with orange has an interesting history, which did not start with the Tour d'Argent, as many people imagine! This almost prototypical French dish is reputedly Italian at source, although there is a good Spanish version local to Seville and the rest of Andalusia, from where today's thin-skinned, sharp-flavoured oranges of the ancient variety come. Oranges reached Europe from China in Roman times, during the first century AD, though it was not until the Arab conquest of Spain in the eighth century that they were grown in any quantity. The marriage of fruit and meat is old beyond calculable time, but I am not going to quarrel with my Italian friends, who adamantly claim that their nation invented this combination with oranges.

Rich Romans, according to Marial, were very partial to duck, and it is quite possible that the Caesars were already eating it with oranges, which at the time would have been an expensive delicacy. The first oranges grown in Europe would have been close in type to today's Seville oranges, but the recipe has changed in degrees of sweetness and sharpness over the centuries, depending on the fashion and taste of each era.

The Florentine recipe for duck or capon with oranges may have reached France with Catherine de Medici when she married the Dauphin and future king Henri II of France in 1533, arriving with an enormous retinue, including cooks who laid the foundations of classic French cuisine. A recipe appears in the earliest fourteenth century Florentine cookbook as *paparo o oca o anitra al melarancia* (gander or goose or duck with orange).

Here is a recipe of Renaissance Florence, as it appears in a book of the period: 'Take a good cold boiled capon. If the capon is roasted, no matter. Cut into small pieces and toss into a pan with half a pound of butter or fat and fry very well. When the capon is well fried, throw on the juice of ten oranges, sugar and cinnamon.' Simple, easy to follow, and a good starting point.

CAPPONE CON SAPORE ARANCIATO
ORANGE-FLAVOURED CAPON

This is an eighteenth-century version of the Florentine dish described on page 68.
Although the recipe is for capon, it is excellent made with duck, or for that matter
guinea fowl, pheasant or partridge.

*bird(s) (see above),
drawn weight about
1.5 kg/3 lb
8 or 10 slices of bacon,
cut as thinly as
possible*

*375 ml/12 fl oz/1 ½
cups dry white wine
2 tablespoons raisins
2 large slices of fresh
white bread without
crusts*

*juice of 6 oranges and
grated zest of 1¼
teaspoon each ground
cinnamon, ginger,
black pepper and
cloves*

*¼ teaspoon saffron,
dissolved in a little
warm water
salt*

Preheat the oven to 180°C/350°F/gas 4. Bard the bird(s) with thin slices of bacon. Roast for about 1 to 1 ½ hours, depending on the bird(s).

When the bacon is browned, pour 250 ml/8 fl oz/1 cup dry white wine over the bird. Baste regularly with the juices as it cooks. Put the raisins to soak in the remaining wine. Soak the bread in the orange juice. Add the grated zest, cinnamon, ginger, pepper, ground cloves and saffron. Pour the rest of the wine into the roasting juices in the pan, and add the mixture of bread and spices, the raisins and the wine in which they have been soaked. Add salt to taste.

Cut the bird into pieces. Place these in an ovenproof casserole just large enough to hold the bird compactly, beat the sauce, pour it over the bird and heat for 5 to 10 minutes, then serve. *Serves 4*

A very similar recipe appears in the Polish section of Audot's *La Cuisinière de la Campagne et de la Ville*, which first appeared in 1818; the last edition, the sixty-fifth, was published in 1887. Audot's capon incorporated onion, carrots, sugar lumps and sharp eating apples as well as the orange juice, but as spices only salt, pepper and 3 cloves.

ITALIAN DUCK IN ORANGE SAUCE: A MODERN VERSION

*1 large duck, about
    3½kg/7 lb undrawn
    (2.75 kg/5½ lb
    drawn)*

*1 tablespoon coarse salt,
    plus more salt as
    needed and black
    pepper
1 tablespoon cornflour*

*250 ml/8 fl oz/1 cup
    chicken consommé
juice of 5 oranges
juice of 1 lemon
3 tablespoons sugar*

*60 ml/2 fl oz/¼ cup
    vinegar
60 ml/2 fl oz/¼ cup
    cognac*

Preheat the oven to 220°C/425°F/gas 7. Wash and dry the duck well. Rub it all over with 1 tablespoon coarse salt and roast for 15 minutes. Lower the heat to 180°C/350°F/gas 4 and cook for about 1¼ hours more (for a bird this size, roasted medium rare).

When cooked cut in 8 portions and arrange these in an ovenproof dish. Keep them warm. Skim off the fat that has collected in the roasting pan. Stir in the cornflour. Place the pan over a low heat. Add the consommé, stirring constantly with a wooden spoon to scrape up any bits of meat that have collected at the bottom. Pour in the orange and lemon juices, sugar and vinegar, and add pepper and more salt if necessary. Cook for a few minutes to reduce the sauce.

When the sauce has become slightly caramelized, pour it over the duck in the ovenproof dish. Warm the cognac gently in a small pan, light it and carefully pour it over the duck. Wait until the flames die down, then serve.
Serves 4

DUCK WITH PINEAPPLE

*1 duck, about 2¾
    kg/5½ lb undrawn
    (2¼ kg/4½ lb
    drawn)*

*salt and black pepper
2 tablespoons butter
180 ml/6 fl oz/¾ cup
    dark rum*

*180 ml/6 fl oz/¾ cup
    unsweetened
    pineapple juice
450 g/15 oz/3 cups*

*fresh pineapple,
    chopped
2 teaspoons arrowroot*

Remove the fat from the cavity of the duck, reserve the giblets and make stock from them. Season the duck with salt and pepper and prick the fatty parts with a fork. Preheat the oven to 160°C/325°F/gas 3.

Brown the duck in the butter in a casserole which is just large enough to hold it. Drain off the fat, and add 120 ml/4 fl oz/½ cup each of dark rum and unsweetened pineapple juice. Bring the mixture to the boil, cover the casserole and roast in the oven for 1½ hours.

Transfer the duck to a platter and keep it warm. Skim off the fat from the casserole and add 250 ml/8 fl oz/1 cup stock made with the reserved giblets and 60 ml/2 fl oz/¼ cup each of unsweetened pineapple juice and dark rum. Reduce the mixture over high heat to about 500 ml/16 fl oz/2 cups.

Strain the liquid into a saucepan, add the chopped pineapple, and cook the mixture over low heat for 5 minutes. Add the arrowroot dissolved in 60 ml/2 fl oz/¼ cup cold water and heat the sauce, stirring, until slightly thickened. Season it with salt and pepper to taste. Serve the duck with the sauce separately.
Serves 4

WILD DUCK WITH ANCHOVIES AND CAPERS

If you have wild duck which have been feeding on the sea coast rather than from inland waters, they may have a slightly fishy taste. In India such birds are cooked in recipes otherwise used for fish (but a Bombay duck is a fish). Here is a recipe with the sharp taste of anchovies and capers, which lends itself well to such birds.

2 wild ducks, about 1¼ kg/2½ lb each
300 ml/10 fl oz/1¼ cups strong dry white wine
6 black peppercorns, slightly crushed, plus

salt and ground black pepper as needed
sprig each of fresh thyme, marjoram and tarragon
a few sprigs of parsley
½ lemon

2 rashers of bacon
1 medium onion, finely chopped
2 tablespoons olive oil
10 anchovy fillets, well drained

60 ml/2 fl oz/¼ cup milk
2 tablespoons chopped capers
2 tablespoons double cream

Marinate the ducks in the wine, peppercorns and herbs for at least 12 hours, turning the birds regularly to ensure even absorption.

Preheat the oven to 200°C/400°F/gas 6. Remove the ducks from the marinade, dry them well, put a piece of lemon inside and bard the breasts with bacon. Roast the ducks for 30 minutes, or until the juices run clear when tested with a skewer.

Fry the onion in the oil until it is transparent. Strain the marinade and add with the chopped anchovies to the onion. Cook until reduced to the consistency of a sauce, then purée it and stir in the capers. Pour off the excess fat from the duck, and add the juices and the cream to the anchovy and caper sauce. Add salt and pepper as necessary. Serve very hot.
Serves 4

ANITRA PORCHETTA
DUCK IN THE STYLE OF SUCKLING PIG

Both duck and chicken are prepared with a filling of *pancetta* (Italian unsmoked, spiced, rolled bacon) and a generously seasoned stuffing, typical of the Italian way of preparing *porchetta* or suckling pig.

Antonio Tempesta's foolproof method of catching ducks is explained in his *Venationes ferarum, avium . . .* (etc), published in Amsterdam in 1627. The hunter disguises himself as a stone, wades into a fast-running river, and reaches up to grab the duck when it lands on the 'stone'. The woodcut illustration shows the 'stone' to be a contraption to fit over the hunter's head, with holes for eyes. Guaranteed to save expenditure on a pair of Purdeys and cold dawns on the Norfolk Broads.

1 large duck, about
  3.5 kg/7 lb undrawn
  (2.75 kg/5½ lb
  drawn)
120 g/4 oz/¼ lb fresh

Italian sausage
90 g/3 oz pancetta or
  an additional 90 g/
  3 oz sausage
2 large bay leaves

1 heaped teaspoon
  rosemary
25 fresh sage leaves
5 large cloves garlic
salt, black peppercorns

and ground black
  pepper
2 generous tablespoons
  olive oil

Remove the sausage from its casing and place the meat in a bowl. Chop the *pancetta* coarsely with the bay leaves, rosemary, 20 of the sage leaves and the garlic. Add this mixture to the sausage meat, then mix in 2 teaspoons salt, 20 whole peppercorns and 1½ teaspoons ground pepper. Make sure it is thoroughly mixed. Preheat the oven to 190°C/375°F/gas 5.

Wash the duck and dry with paper towels. Reserve the liver for another purpose, but do not remove any of the fat. Stuff the duck with the stuffing mixture and sew up with needle and thread. Place the remaining sage leaves in the neck opening and sew this as well.

Remove the rack from the roasting pan and spread olive oil over the bottom of the pan. Put the duck in upside down, sprinkle with salt and pepper and roast for 1 hour, turning often.

Remove the pan from the oven, take the duck out and pour off the fat. Replace the rack in the pan and place the duck on this. Return it to the oven, still at the same temperature, for a further 30 minutes. After cooking allow the duck to settle for 10 or 15 minutes in a warm place, then cut it into pieces. Place the stuffing in the centre of a serving dish surrounded by the duck pieces, and serve with a crisp green salad.
Serves 6

HUNGARIAN ROAST DUCK WITH SOUR CREAM SAUCE

1 duck, about 2¾ kg/5½ lb undrawn (2¼ kg/4½ lb drawn)
36 juniper berries
180 g/6 oz/¾ cup clarified butter
2 teaspoons vinegar
salt and black pepper
2 teaspoons paprika
90 g/3 oz/1½ cups fresh breadcrumbs
250 g/8 oz/2 cups ground hazelnuts
4 teaspoons grated orange zest
130 ml/4½ fl oz/ generous ½ cup sweet sherry
2 medium onions, sliced
500 ml/16 fl oz/2 cups sour cream
4 tablespoons dill weed
2 tablespoons blackcurrant jelly
2 egg yolks
4 tablespoons double cream
2 teaspoons arrowroot

Crush 12 juniper berries and put them with most of the clarified butter in a pan, add the vinegar and season with salt and pepper. Heat gently and allow to infuse. Remove from the heat and add paprika. Set this mixture aside as a glaze for duck. Preheat the oven to 180°C/350°F/gas 4.

Mix the breadcrumbs, hazelnuts and remaining juniper berries with the orange zest and 2 tablespoons sweet sherry. Season with black pepper. Remove the neck of the duck if necessary. Stuff the mixture and truss it. Brush the rack with the remaining clarified butter, and brush the duck with butter glaze. Place it in the oven and allow to roast for about 1 hour 40 minutes.

Remove the duck and keep it warm. Pour the fat from the pan. Add the onions to the pan juices and allow to fry gently for 1 minute or so. Add the remaining sherry, pour into the blender and purée. Sieve the blended mixture into a saucepan and stir in the sour cream, dill and blackcurrant jelly. Mix the egg yolks with cream and arrowroot, and pour it into the sauce. Stir until thickened. Do not let the sauce boil. Serve in a sauceboat.
Serves 4

PEKING DUCK

This spectacular dish is particularly esteemed in China because ordinary households do not have ovens, and you can only have it in a restaurant – originally only the skin of the duck was eaten in the pancakes, while the meat was served in another dish. In order to ensure a crisp, tasty skin, the duck must be hung overnight, preferably in a cool draught. If you have nowhere suitable, you may be able to improvise with an electric fan, or a fan heater or hairdryer which can be set to blow cold air.

Duck is one of the stars of Chinese cuisine, and there is even a special breed of duck reared and fattened to provide it. Some restaurants specialize in duck: the famous Pien Yi Fang restaurant in Peking has more than a hundred duck dishes on its menu, including one of duck's tongues where there are thirty tongues in each serving. The shiny mahogany-coloured ducks hanging in the windows of many Chinese restaurants are a Cantonese speciality. They have a sweet, spicy stuffing made with hoisin and yellow bean sauce, and are glazed with honey, vinegar and food colouring.

1 domestic duck, or 2 wild ducks, total weight about 2½kg/5 lb undrawn (1¾ kg/3½ lb drawn)
1 tablespoonful brandy

PANCAKES:
500 g/1 lb/3 heaped cups plain flour
450 ml/15 fl oz/1¾ cups boiling water
2 tablespoons sesame oil

BASTING SAUCE:
2 tablespoons clear honey
2 tablespoons dark soy sauce
150 ml/5 fl oz/⅔ cup cold water

SAUCE:
4 tablespoons hoisin sauce
¼ teaspoon sesame oil
1 teaspoon clear honey
ACCOMPANIMENTS:
12 spring onions
1 cucumber, shredded

Wash and dry the duck thoroughly. Rub the brandy in well all over the skin. Tie a piece of string under each wing and hang the duck overnight in a cool, dry, airy place.

Next day, begin by removing and discarding the green tops of the spring onions and cutting the main parts in half. Split the upper end of each half into four with a knife. Put the onions into iced water. The split ends will fan out to make a 'brush'.

Then make the pancakes while you preheat the oven to 200°C/400°F/gas 6. Sift the flour into a bowl and stir in the boiling water. Mix to a dough, knead this for a few minutes, then cover it with clingfilm and let it rest for 30 minutes while you carry on with the rest of the recipe.

Mix the basting sauce ingredients together. Put the duck on a rack in a roasting tin which is half filled with cold water. Pour some of the basting sauce over its breast. Roast, breast side up, for 30 minutes, basting every 10 minutes. Then turn the duck, using two wooden spoons, and baste again. The reason for using wooden spoons is so that the skin will not be pierced, as it is important not to let the juices escape. Roast for a further 30 minutes, basting frequently. Turn the duck on to its back and cook for a further 10 minutes, basting.

While the duck is roasting, prepare the pancakes from the dough as soon as it is ready. Knead the dough briefly, divide it in half and keep one half covered. Roll the first half into a sausage shape about 40 cm/16 in long and cut it into 16 equal pieces. Flatten each piece into a 6 cm/2½ in round. Brush half the circles with sesame oil, then press the remaining circles on top of them, making 8 pairs. Make more pancakes with the remaining dough in the same way, to give 16 pairs. Roll out the circles until they measure 15 cm/6 in diameter. Heat a heavy-based frying pan and cook the pancakes in the dry pan for 2 minutes on each side. When ready, the pancake will look dry on the underside and have brown flecks. It will puff when turned over. Remove from the pan, and while still hot, peel the two pieces apart. Keep the pancakes hot wrapped in a cloth or foil.

Mix the accompanying sauce. Remove the skin from the duck and cut it into neat pieces. Use two forks to pull the meat into shreds. Arrange the meat and skin on a serving platter with the spring onions and shredded cucumber around it, and serve the pancakes and accompanying sauce separately.

To eat, spread a little plum sauce over a pancake. Top with spring onion, cucumber, duck and duck skin and roll up. Delicious!
Serves 6

WILD DUCK WITH LENTILS

Many countries have their version of this; French *cassoulet* is one of the family. This is a Middle Eastern version such as might be tasted in Syria or Lebanon. In India, there would be, in addition to these spices, fresh ginger, cloves, finely chopped green chilli, and possible asafoetida. Limes might be used instead of lemons. The dish lends itself to endless permutations.

1 wild duck, about 1¼ kg/2½ lb
4 cloves of garlic, crushed with salt

2 teaspoons each ground coriander, cumin, and cinnamon
1 bay leaf

200 g/7 oz/1 cup lentils, well washed, and drained
salt and black pepper

juice of 2 lemons
chopped fresh coriander for garnish

Simmer the duck with water for 1 hour, until tender. Preheat the oven to 180°C/350°F/gas 4.

Mix the crushed garlic into the cooking liquid, and add the spices and bay leaf. Mix the lentils into this, and cook, uncovered, in the oven until the lentils are soft, about 30 minutes but lentils are very variable.

Adjust the seasoning, adding some lemon juice, and garnish with coriander. Serve the rest of the lemon juice separately for spooning over each portion. A crisp salad and hot flat Eastern bread are all that are required as accompaniments.
Serves 4

FAISANJAN

This is a dish made all over the Middle East. It can be made with chicken, or other
birds, or even with meatballs, but it is best made with duck. It is very rich, and
best served with steamed rice and a side dish of yoghurt. If possible use fresh
pomegranates for the juice – you will need about 4 – but you can get tins of
unsweetened juice or bottles of concentrate from Middle Eastern shops.

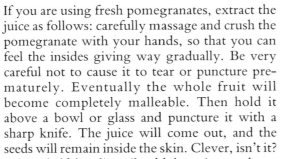

*1 duck, about 2³/4kg/5¹/2
lb undrawn (2¹/4
kg/4¹/2 lb drawn)
150 ml/5 fl oz/²/3 cup
pomegranate juice*

*4 tablespoons olive oil
2 medium onions,
chopped
1 teaspoon turmeric*

*about 500 g/1 lb/2²/3
cups shelled walnuts,
half ground quite fine
and half coarsely
chopped*

*juice of 2 lemons
2 tablespoons sugar, or
to taste
salt and black pepper*

If you are using fresh pomegranates, extract the
juice as follows: carefully massage and crush the
pomegranate with your hands, so that you can
feel the insides giving way gradually. Be very
careful not to cause it to tear or puncture pre-
maturely. Eventually the whole fruit will
become completely malleable. Then hold it
above a bowl or glass and puncture it with a
sharp knife. The juice will come out, and the
seeds will remain inside the skin. Clever, isn't it?

Heat half the olive oil, add the onions and turmeric and cook until the onions are browned.
Transfer them to a heavy casserole, add the walnuts and about 250 ml/8 fl oz/1 cup water, stir

and bring to the boil. Reduce the heat and simmer, covered, for 20 minutes. Meanwhile,
brown the pieces of duck in the remaining oil in
another pan. Transfer the duck to the walnut
mixture and cook, covered, until tender.

Skim as much fat as you can from the top of
the walnut sauce. Add the pomegranate juice,
lemon juice, sugar, salt and pepper to taste, continue simmering, and adjusting the flavour. It
should be sweet-sour. Simmer until the duck is
very tender, probably 1 to 1¹/2 hours. Serve with
a sprinkling of pomegranate seeds on the *faisanjan* and the accompanying rice.
Serves 4-6

DUCK WITH HONEY

This recipe has never failed me. The duck is tender and juicy, and the fat is somehow transformed by the honey into an intense delicious juice. I prefer buckwheat honey for this; it has a distinctive taste which blends well with the spices. A slightly different emphasis can be given to the flavour with a hint of cinnamon (a piece inside the duck, or a little ground cinnamon rubbed into the skin), or with a little fresh ginger.

1 large duck
1 teaspoon fennel seeds

1 teaspoon cumin seeds
twist of lemon peel

1 small onion
salt and black pepper

juice of ½ lemon
2-3 tablespoons clear honey

Prick the duck all over, then leave it in a bowl of hot water for 30 minutes. Grind the fennel and cumin seeds together.

Pat the duck dry, then rub in the ground spices all over. Put the lemon peel and small onion inside the duck, sprinkle with salt and pepper, lay it on foil, then dribble the lemon juice and honey over. Wrap tightly with several layers of foil, so the duck is completely sealed in one place on a baking tray on its side. Roast at 220°C/425°F/gas 7 for 1½-2 hours, turning to other side halfway through cooking.

Serving is a bit tricky. I cut the foil open, turn it back and serve it like that on a large platter. *Serves 4*

DUCK WITH RHUBARB

In Persian cooking, rich stews are often given a piquant edge with sharp fruits. I have already given a recipe for *Faisanjan* (page 76), made with pomegranate juice. Another favourite is a *khoresh* (stew), combining meat and quinces. Here is a version using rhubarb. You can use any meat – lamb is good, as are little meatballs. This recipe uses duck.

1 large duck or 2 or 3 wild duck
2 large onions, chopped
125 g/4 oz/½ cup butter
600 ml/1 pint/2½ cups good stock
juice of 2 lemons
salt and black pepper
2 bunches of fresh parsley, chopped
1 heaped dessertspoon
chopped fresh mint
about 6 stalks rhubarb, chopped

Cut the duck into portions. Sauté the onions in half the butter, and when they have turned golden, add the duck pieces with the stock, lemon juice and seasoning. Cover and simmer for 1 hour.

Meanwhile, in a clean pan, brown the herbs in the remaining butter. Add these to the duck, and continue to simmer gently. Add the rhubarb pieces to the stew for the final 20 minutes cooking time.

Remove the meat to a warm serving dish, skim excess fat from the cooking liquid, and boil it to reduce and intensify the flavours. Pour the sauce over the duck pieces before serving. Serve with hot, cooked basmati rice.

Serves 4

SNIPE WITH PAPRIKA AND SOUR CREAM

Snipe live in marshy terrain. They are a little larger than woodcock, but similar in
taste, with rich dark meat and a distinctive flavour. When roasted, their long beak
is turned to skewer the legs. I believe some people like the beaks roasted and
toasted crisp, to eat like a cocktail snack, but my mind boggles at the idea of
having such a large bag of snipe that this would be possible. This is a modest
recipe, for one person! Multiply as quantities and snipe (one per head) permit.

1 snipe, stuffed with a   *3 tablespoons butter*   *1 teaspoon paprika*   *150 ml/5 fl oz/²⁄₃ cup*
*   bacon roll*   *1 medium onion, thinly*   *½ teaspoon dried thyme*   *   soured cream*
seasoned flour, to dredge   *   sliced in rings*

Dredge the bird in seasoned flour, then sauté in
the butter. Place it in an ovenproof dish, lay the
onion rings on top, sprinkle with paprika and
thyme. Pour the soured cream over, cover with
a lid or foil, and roast at 120°C/325°F/gas 3 for
about 35 minutes. If you object to meat on the
rare side, cook for one hour.

SWAN

In past centuries swan and peacock were served at royal banquets, with their skins sewn back over the cooked meat, tails spread, and head and neck propped erect with a spike inside. The appearance was undoubtedly spectacular. The meat of both these birds is dark.

A Swan Feast is still traditionally held each November at the Vintners' Hall in the City of London. Wild swans in Britain belong to the Crown, or to the Dyers' Company or the Vintners' Company, and they are ceremonially marked each year at the Swan-Upping Cere-

mony on the river Thames. Unmarked swans belong to the Crown; those of the companies are marked with nicks on their beaks, one nick for the Dyers and two nicks for the Vintners.

Nowadays the central dish of the feast is usually goose, and any swan or cygnet served is one which has met a natural, accidental death during the course of the year (through flying into telegraph wires, for example) and has been preserved for the feast by deep freezing. The caterers who prepare the feast told me that they normally serve the birds roasted, and sometimes include smoked goose as well.

A TRADITIONAL RECIPE FOR ROAST SWAN, WITH CASHEW NUT STUFFING

1 cygnet or young swan, about 4 kg/8 lb	*120 g/4 oz/⅔ cup pine nuts*	*grated zest of 1 lemon*	*flour*
500 g/1 lb/2⅔ cups cashew nuts	*1 kg/2 lb sausage meat*	*1 teaspoon thyme*	*300 g/10 oz/1¼ cups lard*
	1 onion, chopped	*salt and black pepper*	
		2½ kg/5 lb/20 cups	*1.2 l/2 pints/5 cups water*

Mix the nuts, sausage meat, onion and seasonings together, and stuff the bird with this forcemeat. Preheat the oven to 200°C/400°F/gas 6. Make a stiff dough with the flour, lard and water, roll it out to a thickness 6 mm/¼ in/¼ in

and wrap the bird in this, sealing the edges of the dough with a little water. Put it in a baking tin and roast in the oven for 2½ to 3 hours.

Serve with an orange and chicory salad.
Serves 10-12

LARGE FURRED GAME

DEER

Durham Cathedral was founded on the site of an ancient deer shrine. Its name was originally Duirholm, the Meadow of the Deer, and it was a place of pagan pilgrimage many centuries before it was made Christian and a church was built there. Deer were always considered magical as well as useful. The Celtic woodland goddess Flidhais often appeared as a hind, and we have stories of magical white hinds appearing in medieval legends. There are the magical stags of St Hubert and St Eustace which appeared with the Crucifixion set between their antlers, and the no less believable and symbolic story of Artemis and Actaeon. The famous stag-man of the Les Trois Frères cave paintings suggests a stag cult more than fourteen thousand years ago, and stag masks and horns are symbols of many shamanistic cults. The ancient Scythians believed that the stag was the mount which would carry dead heroes to the other world, and sacrificed horses in graves are often decorated with antlers made from stitched and stuffed felt mounted on leather headdresses.

BISTECCA ALLA CACCIATORA
HUNTER'S STEAK

1 large venison steak, about 500 g/1 lb	2 cloves of garlic, chopped 1 sprig of rosemary	2 tablespoons oil 100 ml/3½ fl oz/⅓ cup dry white wine	2 large tomatoes, peeled and seeded salt and black pepper

Fry the garlic and rosemary in oil. When the garlic is golden remove it from the pan and add the meat, browning both sides over high heat. Moisten with the wine, and after this has evaporated add the tomatoes and cook gently for about 20 minutes or until tender then season, and serve.
Serves 2

BROAD BEANS AND MINCED VENISON

This is a Middle Eastern dish.

The edible entrails of a deer are known as umbles. These used to be made into a pie, usually a 'below stairs' provision, which gave occasion to the expression 'eating humble pie'. The entrails were cooked with ginger, nutmeg, dates, raisins and currants, then baked in a pastry crust in the oven.

1 kg/2 lb/6 cups fresh broad beans (weight without pods)
750 g/1½ lb minced
venison
6 tablespoons olive oil
salt and black pepper
½ teaspoon dried thyme,
or more to taste
2 teaspoons mixed ground spices – nutmeg, cinnamon,
cayenne pepper, ground cloves
3 eggs
lemon juice to taste

If you like, skin the beans. Put them in a pan with 4 tablespoons of oil and just enough water to cover them. Sprinkle with salt, pepper and thyme. Simmer them gently until they are tender, adding a little water if necessary.

Meanwhile, in a separate pan heat 2 tablespoons of oil, add the spices and seasonings and then stir in the venison. When this is cooked and soft, add it to the beans and stir well. Break the eggs into a little bowl, whisk lightly with a fork, then pour these into the pan. Cook, stirring constantly, until the eggs have cooked. Turn it out into a serving dish and let it cool.

Adjust the seasoning and serve cold, sprinkled with lemon juice.
Serves 4

VENISON AND KUMQUAT PASTIES

I have suggested pickled kumquats, but fresh ones can be used equally well. Remove the pips, slice, and reserve some whole fruits for garnish. The texture of pickled walnuts goes well as an accompanying chutney.

300 g/10 oz/2¼ cups cooked venison, coarsely minced
pastry made with 200 g/ scant 7 oz/1½ cups self-raising and plain flours and 200 g/ 7 oz/scant 1 cup lard
1 medium onion,
chopped
1 tablespoon butter, plus more to grease baking sheet
120 g/4 oz/1⅔ cups mushrooms (wild if possible, chanterelles if you can get them), chopped
1 tablespoon Madeira
120 g/4 oz/1⅔ cups cooked wild rice (cooked weight)
6 pickled kumquats, seeds removed, chopped
1 tablespoon mushroom ketchup
4 juniper berries, crushed
½ teaspoon ground allspice
¼ teaspoon ground cinnamon
salt and black pepper
a little stock, if needed
1 egg yolk, beaten

Start by making the pastry. Wrap it in clingfilm and leave it in the refrigerator to rest while you make the filling.

Cook the onion in 1 tablespoon butter until it is transparent. Add the mushrooms and Madeira, and when the mushrooms are soft add the cooked and drained wild rice, venison, kumquats, mushroom ketchup, juniper berries, spices, salt and pepper. Taste and adjust the seasoning. If the mixture seems dry, moisten it with a little stock.

Roll the pastry out about 3 mm/⅛ in thick and cut it into circles of about 14 cm/5 in diameter. It should make at least 16 circles. Preheat the oven to 200°C/400°F/gas 6.

Put a good spoonful of filling in the middle of each pastry circle, dampen the edges, and crimp it together with your fingers, either by turning both edges up and joining them at the top, or by pulling one side right over and pressing it down on the other. Brush the pasties with beaten egg, prick them with a fork, and cook them on a buttered baking sheet for 10 to 15 minutes. Serve these hot, warm or cold, with chutney and a crisp salad.
Serves 4

VENISON CHILLI

Chilli powder is often not simply powdered hot peppers, but a mixture of spices. Its strength varies enormously, so add it carefully.

1 kg/2 lb minced venison
1 large onion, chopped
3 cloves of garlic, chopped
1 tablespoon diced fatty bacon
1½-2 tablespoons chilli powder, or 1 teaspoon cayenne pepper
1 teaspoon ground cumin
1 teaspoon dried oregano
250 g/8 oz/1 cup tinned tomato purée (use less and dilute if triple concentrated)
250 ml/8 fl oz/1 cup stock or water
juice of ½ lemon and ½ teaspoon grated zest
1 teaspoon brown sugar
salt and black pepper
800 g/1 lb 10 oz/4⅓ cups cooked red kidney beans (cooked weight – may be tinned)

Sauté the onion and garlic with the bacon, and when it has started to change colour add the meat and brown it. Add the chilli powder, cumin and oregano and continue to cook, stirring, for 5 minutes. Add the tomato purée, stir well, then mix in the stock or water, lemon juice and zest, sugar, salt and pepper. Simmer for 1 to 1½ hours.

Add the beans and adjust the seasoning before you serve. Hot crusty garlic bread and a crunchy salad make this a filling meal.
Serves 6

SHURA'S SHOULDER OF YOUNG VENISON

Shura (Alexander Schewarg) is the man behind the Golden Duck restaurant in Chelsea. A wonderful, crazy Russian who grew up in China, he generously gave me time and help with a few of my areas of ignorance. Here is one of his recipes. You can use a piece of haunch instead of shoulder, and farmed venison is as suitable as wild.

Another way of preparing this recipe is to brown the meat with the cardamom, cinnamon and butter, then seal it in several layers of tightly wrapped foil with the Madeira, cherry juice, stock and butter, and continue to roast it at the original high temperature.

1 shoulder of venison, about 3 kg/6 lb with bone
salt and black pepper
500 g/1 lb/3 cups fresh sour cherries
60 g/2 oz/¼ cup butter
3 or 4 cardamom pods
50 ml/1¾ fl oz/3⅓
1 teaspoon ground cinnamon
1 tablespoon flour
tablespoons Madeira
100 ml/3½ fl oz/⅓ cup stock

Wash the venison and salt it slightly. You may remove the bone. Preheat the oven to 200°C/400°F/gas 6.

Stone 20 or 30 of the cherries and squeeze the others to yield about 50 ml/1¾ fl oz/3⅓ tablespoons juice. Make incisions all over the meat as for garlic, and into each incision put a stoned cherry. Put the meat in a casserole and dot it with the seeds, a little of the butter, the seeds from the cardamom pods, and a spoonful of ground cinnamon. Set it in the oven, uncovered, to brown.

When the meat is browned reduce the heat to 180°C/350°F/gas 4. Sprinkle the meat with flour through a sieve, put the lid on and return it to the oven. A piece this size will take about 2 hours in all to cook. When it is half cooked add the Madeira, cherry juice and stock, and the rest of the butter, and let it continue cooking. Baste frequently. Correct the seasoning before serving.
Serves 6

VENISON CIDER STEW

This recipe is adapted from one in *Gourmet* magazine.

1.5 kg/3 lb boned
   shoulder or rump of
   venison
500 ml/16 fl oz/2 cups
   cider, preferably
   rough
12 allspice berries,

crushed
12 black peppercorns,
   crushed, and more
   ground pepper
8 sprigs of parsley, tied
   in a bunch
1 teaspoon rosemary,

crushed
salt
250 g/8 oz/½ lb bacon,
   in a piece
4 tablespoons butter
3 tablespoons flour
1 medium onion,

chopped
2 large carrots, diced
2 stalks celery, chopped
300 ml/10 fl oz/1¼
   cups brown stock or
   beef broth
1 bay leaf

Cut the meat into 2.5 cm/1 in cubes and put it in a bowl with the cider, allspice, peppercorns, parsley, rosemary and 1 teaspoon of salt. Let it marinate, turning occasionally, for 12 hours.

Blanch the bacon in water to cover for 5 minutes, dry it with paper towels, and cut it into 1 cm/½ in cubes. Sauté these in 3 tablespoons butter until crisp, and transfer with a slotted spoon to paper towels to drain.

Drain the venison, reserving the marinade, dry it with paper towels, and dredge it with about 2 tablespoons flour seasoned with salt and pepper. Pour all but 60 ml/2 fl oz/¼ cup fat from the pan but retain. Brown the venison, one batch at a time, in the remaining fat over a moderately high heat, adding more fat if necessary, then transfer it to a flameproof casserole.

Preheat the oven to 160°C/325°F/gas 3. In the same fat sauté the onion, carrots and celery until the vegetables are softened. Add the vegetables, marinade, stock and bay leaf to the casserole and bring the liquid to a boil. Transfer the stew to the oven and cook, covered, for 1½ hours or until the meat is tender.

Remove the parsley and bay leaf, skim off the fat and transfer the venison with slotted spoon to a heated serving dish. Mix the remaining table-spoonfuls of butter and flour to make a *beurre manié* and stir this into the cooking liquid. Boil until reduced to a rich sauce, correct the season-ing, pour over the venison and serve.

Serves 6-8

CHINESE AROMATIC SPICED VENISON

1.5 kg/3 lb boned
  venison
2½ l/4 pints/2½ quarts
  water

6 star anise heads
2½ cm/1 in fresh ginger,
  chopped
5 tablespoons dark soy

sauce
5 tablespoons sugar
2 tablespoons salt
3 tablespoons dry sherry

(or shao hsing wine if
  available)
fresh coriander leaves or
  flat-leaf parsley for
  garnish

Trim any membrane from the meat. Bring the water to the boil and add the anise and ginger, then put in the meat. Cover and simmer for 1 hour. Add the soy sauce, sugar and salt, cover again and cook for another ½ hour. Add the sherry and cook, uncovered, over medium heat, turning the meat in the sauce as it continues to cook. Cook about 40 minutes or until the meat is tender and there is about 250 ml/8 fl oz/1 cup of sauce remaining.

Transfer the meat to a casserole and strain the sauce into a saucepan. Let both cool, then cover and refrigerate. The sauce will set to a jelly.

Cut the meat into thick slices and arrange them on a platter. Cut the jelly into cubes and arrange the pieces over the meat. Garnish and serve.

Serves 6-8

SIBERIAN *SHASHLIK*

Shashlik is a dish associated more with Turkey than Siberia, but the idea of cooking meat on skewers is widespread. Hamburg parsley is a favourite flavouring in Russian cooking. It is a form of parsley with a large root, and the root is used rather than the leaves. It sometimes appears in my local Portobello market. If you cannot find it, substitute celeriac.

1 kg/2 lb boned venison
125 g/4 oz/⅔ cup
  onion, chopped
1 small green pepper,
  chopped
120 g/4 oz/¼ lb
  Hamburg parsley

root, chopped
100 ml/3½ fl oz/⅓ cup
  oil
50 ml/2 fl oz/¼ cup
  cognac
salt and black pepper

1 large (397 g/14 oz)
  tin of tomatoes
1 small bunch spring
  onions
juice of ½ lemon
1 clove of garlic, finely
  chopped

1 tablespoon tomato
  purée
1 tablespoon fresh dill
1 teaspoon cayenne
  pepper

Make a marinade with onions, green pepper, Hamburg parsley, oil, cognac, salt and pepper. Cut the venison into bite-sized pieces and marinate for 10 to 12 hours.

Dry the pieces and thread them on skewers. Combine the tomatoes, spring onions, lemon juice, garlic, tomato purée, dill and cayenne in a saucepan over a low heat to make a sauce. Cook this until it becomes thick. Meanwhile, grill the meat. Season the sauce with salt and pepper and serve with the *shashlik*.

Serves 4

SAPHED MANS
WHITE MEAT

This recipe takes its name from the colour of the ingredients. I learned it from His Highness Arvind Singh Mewar, sitting in the courtyard of the Shiv Niwas Palace, Udaipur. Whatever I know of Indian cooking was learnt in Udaipur, and I am sure that the cooks groan when they see me arrive each year, and celebrate when I leave!

500 g/1 lb boned venison
salt
120 g/4 oz/½ cup ghee (clarified butter)
120 g/4 oz/½ cup yoghurt

1 tablespoon chilli powder
1 tablespoon shredded ginger root
1 tablespoon ground almonds

12 white poppy seeds
1 tablespoon shredded or ground coconut (fresh if possible; otherwise use coconut cream)
120 ml/4 fl oz/½ cup milk

few drops of rosewater
squeeze of fresh lime juice
pinch of cardamom seeds, crushed

Bring the meat to boiling point in a pan of salted water. After 5 minutes, pour off the water and rinse the meat thoroughly.

Heat the ghee and add the meat with the yoghurt, chilli seeds and ginger and about 50 ml/1¾ fl oz/3⅓ tablespoons water. Then add the almonds, poppy seeds, coconut and milk, and stir. Cover the pan and simmer until the meat is tender (the time depends on the age of the animal). By then the gravy should have thickened and the ghee be floating on top. Add the rosewater, lime juice and ground cardamom, and serve with plain boiled rice.

Serves 4

VENISON PULAO

1 kg/2 lb venison,
    including bones
4 cm/1½ in fresh ginger,
    finely chopped
8 cloves of garlic,
    crushed
175 g/6 oz/¾ cup ghee
    (clarified butter)

4 large onions, finely
    chopped
1 teaspoon red chilli
    powder or paste (less,
    if you are nervous
    about making it too
    hot)
8 cloves

4 black cardamom pods
5 cm/2 in stick of
    cinnamon
1 teaspoon of lightly
    crushed cumin
1 teaspoon turmeric
600 ml/2 pint/2½ cups
    stock or water

500 g/1 lb/2⅔ cups
    long grain rice (eg
    basmati), well
    washed
1 tablespoon of fresh
    lemon juice
salt to taste

Marinate the meat for a least an hour in a mixture of crushed ginger and garlic. Heat half the ghee, then add the onions and spices except for turmeric. When the onions have turned colour, add the turmeric and the meat, including the garlic and ginger marinade. Cook gently, adding a little of the stock or water to prevent it from drying out.

When the meat is tender, heat the remaining ghee in a large pan, then pour the well washed rice into this. Let it absorb the ghee, then add stock, or water, or a mixture of stock and water, to a level almost 5 cm/2 in above the rice. Mix well, add a tablespoon of fresh lemon juice, and bring to a simmer. Add the meat, and continue to cook gently until the rice has absorbed the liquid and is tender.

A hearty dish for 4 to 6 people

POLISH MARINATED ELK WITH *PEPPER SAUCE*

Allow 250 g/8 oz/½ lb meat per person

fillet of elk (or venison)
fatty bacon for larding
marinade ('general',
    'strong' or 'cooked',
    according to age of
    animal – see pages 15
    and 152

fines herbes (mixture of
    fresh parsley, chervil,
    chives and a little
    tarragon)
fresh breadcrumbs for
    coating
butter for sprinkling

PEPPER SAUCE:
1 medium onion,
    chopped
2 tablespoons butter
250 ml/8 fl oz/1 cup
    brown game stock
120 ml/4 fl oz/½ cup

dry red wine
1 tablespoon black
    peppercorns, crushed
1 tablespoon redcurrant
    jelly
2 teaspoons flour

Lard the meat with the bacon and marinate it for 3 days, turning occasionally.

Preheat the oven to 180°C/350°F/gas 4. Roast the meat, uncovered, until it is three-quarters cooked (the time will depend on age and size), then cut it into thickish slices and reassemble the pieces to the original form by putting a thick mixture of *fines herbes* between each slice. Coat the whole thing with the same herb mixture, then sprinkle it with breadcrumbs and melted butter and return it to the oven until the coating is browned and the meat fully cooked.

Meanwhile, make a pepper sauce – for a large piece of meat double the quantities given above. Sauté the onion gently in 1 teaspoon butter until lightly browned. Add the stock, wine, peppercorns and redcurrant jelly and bring to the boil. Mix the remaining butter with the flour to make a *beurre manié* and stir this thoroughly into the sauce. Cook until the sauce is quite thick.

Serve the meat with potatoes and the sauce in a sauceboat.

SLOTTSTEK
PALACE STEAK

1.1 kg/2¼ lb boned venison	*4 anchovy fillets, drained and chopped*	*4 cloves*	SAUCE:
2 tablespoons butter	*1 tablespoon black treacle or molasses*	*salt, 5 whole white peppercorns and a little ground white pepper*	*150 ml/5 fl oz/⅔ cup juices from the roast*
2 medium onions, chopped	*1 tablespoon vinegar*		*2 tablespoons plain flour*
150 ml/5 fl oz/⅔ cup stock	*2 bay leaves*		*8-10 tablespoons double cream*
	8 allspice berries		*salt and white pepper*

Preheat the oven to 190°C/375°F/gas 5. Melt the butter and brown the meat. Remove the meat and keep it warm on one side while you allow the chopped onions to become transparent in the butter. Add the rest of the main ingredients, and put the meat in this liquid into a heavy oven-proof dish with a tight-fitting lid. Cook it in the oven for 30 minutes, then turn the meat and stir the sauce around in the dish. Replace the lid and return the dish to the oven. Do this once or twice more over a period of about 1½ hours.

Check that the meat is tender, and if so remove it to a warm serving dish and prepare the sauce. Scrape the bits sticking round the cooking pot, and reduce the cooking liquid until about 450 ml/15 fl oz/scant 2 cups liquid remains. Tip the dish, and put 2 tablespoons flour in the uppermost, drier corner. Stir this, and gradually add the reduced liquid. Cook it over a fairly high heat so that you get rid of any potential lumps and have a smooth sauce. Add the cream and adjust the seasoning.

Carve the meat, and serve it with some of the cream sauce poured over it, and the rest served separately in a sauceboat.
Serves 3

This Swedish recipe was originally for elk, but is thoroughly suitable for any venison, or even beef or veal. The correct kind of anchovies to use is a Swedish brand in lobster sauce, which come in a big pink tin marked 'Abbas Grebbeshad's hummer ansjovis'. If you are lucky enough to find these, add some of the lobster sauce to the recipe. If not, never mind: ordinary anchovy fillets will do perfectly well.

KIBBEH WITH GAZELLE

There are many regional versions of *kibbeh* or *koubba* all across the Middle East. It is an ancient dish, and very much part of the staple diet of the Fertile Crescent. *Kibbeh* are made in many shapes, but they all incorporate a mixture of *burghul* (parched, cracked wheat), minced meat, onion and herbs. Usually, as here, the meat is lamb; in this recipe gazelle is used in the filling. This is the simplest version to make, as it does not require the practised finger techniques needed to make the classic torpedo-shaped stuffed *kibbeh*. Since gazelle are rather thin on the ground in Europe and America, substitute venison; tender farmed venison is perfect, and could also be used in the main *kibbeh* mixture if you prefer.

250 g/8 oz/1⅓ cups burghul, soaked and rinsed
1 large onion, finely grated
250 g/8 oz/½ lb lean lamb, very finely minced to a paste
grated zest of 1 lemon

generous handful of chopped parsley
1 teaspoon ground cumin
1 teaspoon ground coriander
salt and black pepper
6 tablespoons butter
about 120 ml/4 fl oz/½ cup stock

FILLING:
250 g/8 oz/½ lb gazelle (or venison), minced
1 medium onion, finely chopped
2 tablespoons olive oil
120 g/4 oz/⅔ cup pine nuts
120 g/4 oz/⅔ cup

walnuts, coarsely chopped
a few tablespoon stock or water
1 scant teaspoon ground cinnamon
¼ teaspoon ground allspice
salt and black pepper

Start by making the filling. Fry the onion in hot oil until it is golden and soft. Add the meat and nuts and continue to cook gently until the meat is well browned and crumbly. Add a few tablespoons of water or stock to soften the meat, and add the spices and salt and pepper to taste.

Preheat the oven to 180°C/350°F/gas 4. Mix all the other ingredients together except the butter and stock. Use 2 tablespoons of the butter to grease a baking tray. Smooth half the mixture across the bottom of the baking tray. Spread the filling evenly over this, and cover with a second layer of mixture. Press down well, and cut dia-

gonal lines to make diamond shapes.

Melt 3 tablespoons butter and pour this all over the top of the *kibbeh*. Bake it in the oven for 15 minutes, then baste with stock. Continue cooking, basting occasionally, for 1 hour. About 5 minutes before cooking is completed, dot the remaining 1 tablespoon butter over the top, and crisp the surface, either by turning the heat up or placing the *kibbeh* under the grill.

Serve the *kibbeh* with thick yoghurt, which may also be mixed with garlic, mint and cucumber.
Serves 4

KENYAN GAZELLE WITH MANGOES AND CASHEW NUTS

Again, this is excellent made with venison.

1 rack of gazelle, about 1.2 kg/2½ lb (or about 900 g/1¾ lb boned venison)
salt and black pepper

175 g/6 oz unsalted bacon, thinly sliced
4 tablespoons oil
2 small mangoes
2 tablespoons butter

200 g/7 oz/heaped 1 cup unsalted cashew nuts
250 ml/8 fl oz/1 cup dry red wine

3 tablespoons cranberries
2 tablespoons cognac
120 ml/4 fl oz/½ cup stock
1 teaspoon cornflour (if needed)

Preheat the oven to 230°C/450°F/gas 8. Season the rack of gazelle lightly with salt and pepper. Cover it with slices of bacon and bind with string. Heat the oil in a large roasting pan. Put the rack in the pan and roast in the oven for 20 minutes. Remove the bacon and return rack to oven for another 20 minutes to brown.

While the rack is in the oven, cut the mangoes in half and remove the flesh, keeping the half skins intact and reserving them. Dice the flesh. Heat the butter in a frying pan and add the mango and cashew nuts. Deglaze with half the red wine and simmer. Place the mango shells on a serving dish.

Remove the rack from the oven and drain off the oil. Add the cranberries to the pan and deglaze with the remaining red wine and cognac. Simmer for 2 minutes. Add the stock. Simmer for another 5 minutes and season to taste. The sauce should be slightly reduced and thickened. If it is not thick enough, stir in 1 teaspoon cornflour mixed to a paste with the little water.

Fill mango shells with mango and cashew nut mixture and arrange around the carved rack on a large dish. Serve with noodles, and hand the cranberry sauce separately.

Serves 4

Gervase Markham gives detailed instructions in *The English House-Wife* (1615) as to which meats need a gentle heat to be 'pale and white rosted' with a brisk flame, while others – swans, peacocks, bustards, mutton – require slow, steady gentle cooking. Dry meats like venison 'will lie long at the fire and soak well in the rosting'. He also describes the large cold pies which were kept on the sideboard for serving, and were filled with 'red deer, venison, wild boar, gammons of bacon, swans, elkes, porpus and such like'.

WILD BOAR

The Eastern taboo on eating pig's flesh has nothing to do with trichinosis or other illnesses. The pig taboo was copied by early Hebrews from Syria and Egypt, where pigs were sacred to the Great Goddess and were eaten only on ceremonial occasions. The custom was widely known throughout the Mediterranean and Middle East, where the pig was a totem animal. It was sacred in Germanic and Celtic mythology, and in both branches of the ancient Indo-Aryan worship of Vishnu as the boar god. Among the Rajputs of Rajasthan, the boar was sacred to Goori, the corn goddess, and was ceremonially hunted on horseback with spears at the start of the hunting season. The participants wore green. The Celts associated the pig with the other world, and ate pork at feasts only. The Christmas boar's head with an apple in its mouth dates back to the Norse Yule pig sacrifice at the turn of the year.

Small wonder, when you consider what an impressive, even terrifying, animal the boar is. I vividly remember the first time I saw one. It was in Paris, where I lived for some months with my daughter Chloe, then aged nine. Part of life's pleasure was the local market, erected on certain days, its array of fresh produce beautifully displayed on stalls which vanished by early evening. Decisions to purchase had to be taken early in the morning, and competition was loud, fiere and bustling. There, hanging outside a butcher, was something quite extraordinary. My immediate thought was: could it be a bear? Bristly, brindled, and aggressive even in death, it seemed quite unrelated to the naked pink domestic pigs beside which it hung.

The European wild boar is still occasionally hunted. Recently it has been reintroduced to Britain, where it is commercially raised but definitely not allowed to return to the wild. The French distinguish between adult wild boar, *sanglier*, and young boar, *marcassin*. The latter is a much sought-after treat, and if it appears on a restaurant menu, do make a bee-line for it.

The European wild boar was introduced to the United States earlier this century. The native American wild pig is the peccary or *javelina*, a smaller animal, which ranges all the way from the South American countries to Mexico and the south western states. In some parts of America there are razorbacks, domestic pigs which have lived and bred wild, and reverted to an energetic earlier type.

All members of the pig family, wild or domestic, are intelligent and can be extremely dangerous, and a boar hunt is a serious undertaking. The boar spear formerly used in medieval Europe was provided with a crosspiece on the shaft behind the head, since the speared animal was quite capable of running up the shaft and mauling the hunter.

Wild pigs forage by rooting, and their whereabouts is discovered by looking for signs of their feeding areas. They have a great ability to locate buried food by smell – hence the use of domestic pigs in truffle hunting in the Bordeaux and Périgord areas of France. In Africa they cause havoc in the groundnut plantations, which are often owned and run by Muslims who have no use for the pig in any form. Here, wild pig can be obtained for the price of the bullets used to shoot it – or so I am told by a Portuguese friend who used to buy pigs in this way.

POTACCIO DI CINGHIALE
WILD BOAR STEW

This is an adaptation of a Renaissance recipe. The swampy forest lands of the Maremma, the formerly wild coast between Rome and Pisa, once abounded in boar which was highly appreciated by the Florentines. Sportsmen still hunt for boar in this area, although the supply today is much diminished. Those who live in parts of the world where this delicacy is not obtainable can substitute lean loin of pork.

1 kg/2 lb lean meat	*onions, chopped*	*250 ml/8 fl oz/1 cup*	*a little beef consommé,*
1 bottle dry red wine	*2 tablespoons olive oil*	*Marsala*	*if needed*
2 tablespoons flour	*salt*	*250 g/8 oz/1⅓ cups*	
500 g/1 lb/2½ cups	*cayenne pepper*	*ripe quinces, diced*	

Cut the meat into 2½ cm/1 in cubes, cover with red wine and leave in a cool place for 3 days. (For domestic pork 1 day would suffice.)

Remove the meat from the marinade (reserve this), dry the pieces thoroughly and flour them. Sauté the chopped onions in olive oil until pale gold. Add the meat, and turn constantly until browned. Season with salt and cayenne. Pour on the Marsala and add the diced quinces. The tart-

ness of the quinces produces the famous Italian *agrodolce*, a mild sweet-and-sour flavour.

Place all the ingredients, including the marinade, in a large cast iron or earthenware casserole with a tight-fitting lid. Simmer gently for 1 hour. Remove the lid and continue to simmer for a further 1 hour. If the meat becomes dry, add a little heated beef consommé.
Serves 4

RUSSIAN BRAISED WILD BOAR

There are several Russian dishes where the meat is 'larded' with vegetables – slivers of different vegetables and herbs are inserted into knife punctures in the meat, just as we are accustomed to doing with garlic or bacon fat. If you cannot find Hamburg parsley (see page 86), substitute about 120 g/4 oz/1 cup celeriac for both this and the celery.

700 g/1 lb 6 oz meat
1 root Hamburg parsley
2 sticks of celery

400 ml/14 fl oz/1¾ cups 'general' marinade (see page 15)

150 ml/5 fl oz/⅔ cup dry red wine
2 onions, sliced
1 medium carrot, sliced

50 g/1¾ oz/3⅓ tablespoons pork lard
1 tablespoon flour
salt and black pepper

Lard the meat with slivers of Hamburg parsley root and celery. Put this in a ceramic or enamel – not bare metal – dish, and pour the marinade over it. Leave it in a cold place for a least 2 days.

During the 2 days make a stock from the boar's bones, red wine, onions and carrots.

Remove the meat and dry the pieces, then fry them in the lard, pack them into a deep pan, and cover with stock. Cover this and cook gently over a very low heat until the meat is tender –

probably about 2 hours.

Remove the meat with a slotted spoon, and thicken the sauce with the flour, stirring well. When the sauce has a good texture, season with salt and pepper and strain it. Cut the meat against the grain into thick slices, and serve it with roast potatoes, braised cabbage, and the sauce poured over the meat.

Serves 4

CINGHIALE BRASATO
BRAISED WILD BOAR

1 kg/2 lb boar or lean pork
1 bottle dry white wine, or more if needed
2 large carrots (1 sliced, 1 whole)

2 large onions, (1 sliced, 1 whole)
2 sticks celery (1 chopped, 1 whole)
1 tablespoon black peppercorns, and

some ground pepper
50 g/2 oz pancetta (or dry-cured belly of pork)
30 ml/1 fl oz/2 tablespoons olive oil

30 g/1 oz/2 tablespoons butter
1 small bunch parsley
about 250 ml/8 fl oz/ 1 cup stock
salt

Marinate the meat for 1 or 2 days (depending on the age of the animal) in enough white wine to cover it completely, with the sliced carrot, sliced onion, chopped celery and peppercorns. If you can, reserve 100 ml/3½ fl oz/⅓ cup wine for the next stage of the recipe. If you use pork, marinate it for 12 hours only.

Remove the meat from marinade, pat it dry, make cuts in the surface and insert pieces of *pancetta*, cut coarsely and coated with pepper. Fry the meat lightly in the oil and butter. When all sides are golden, add 100 ml/3½ fl oz/3⅓ cup dry white wine to the pan. When this has evaporated add the whole carrot, onion, celery and parsley tied in a bundle so that they do not dissolve in the sauce and can be easily removed at the last moment. Lower the heat to a gentle simmer, cover with a lid and cook until tender, moistening with stock from time to time. Wild boar may take 2 hours, pork less.

Remove the meat and carve it into slices. Reduce the sauce until fairly thick and season. Pour it over the meat or serve separately.
Serves 4

SFOGLIATA
LAYERED PIE WITH CRACKLING

This is a traditional pie made in Bari. It does not have anything specific to do with wild boar as opposed to domestic pig, but I have included it because it is good.

1 kg/2 lb/8 cups flour	(tinned plum	a small tin)	chopped
2 teaspoons salt	tomatoes are good)	3 eggs, hard-boiled and	50 g/1¾ oz/3⅓
6 medium onions	4 tablespoons olive oil	sliced	tablespoons hard
1 tablespoon ricotta	4 or 5 tablespoons pork	60 g/2 oz/¼ cup black	pecorino cheese,
cheese	crackling	olives, stoned	grated
2 well-flavoured	100 g/3½ oz fresh tuna,	2 salted anchovies,	black pepper
tomatoes, crushed	cooked and flaked (or	boned, washed and	

Make a fairly stiff unleavened dough with the flour, salt and some water. Knead until it is elastic, then roll into two large discs about 30 cm/12 in/12 in across.

Slice the onions lengthwise and fry them with the ricotta and tomatoes in 2 tablespoons oil. When half fried add the crackling and pieces of tuna. Leave to cook gently for 5 minutes. Preheat the oven to 200°C/400°F/gas 6.

Lay one disc in a large baking sheet greased with half the remaining oil, spread the fried mixture over it, then make a layer of sliced hard boiled eggs, followed by the stoned olives, chopped anchovies and grated *pecorino* cheese. Add pepper to taste. Cover with the other disc of dough, seal the edges, brush the surface with the rest of the oil and bake for 30 minutes.
Serves 4-6.

NEW MEXICO WILD BOAR SPARE RIBS WITH *CHIPOTLE* AND PEANUT SAUCE

Chipotle are smoke-cured *jalapeños*, which are a fairly serious kind of hot pepper. If you can't find *chipotles*, you can used canned *jalapeños*. Check the heat as you go: there is no point in making something too hot to eat, and people's tastes differ. Needless to say, this recipe can be made with ordinary American-cut spare ribs of pork.

2-3 kg/4-6 lb spare ribs
salt and black pepper
120 g/4 oz/¾ cup
* tinned tomato purée*

(use less and dilute if
* triple concentrated)*
a little bottled chilli
* sauce, to taste*

4 chipotles
2 tablespoons brown
* sugar or honey*
2 tablespoons cider
* vinegar*

90 g/3 oz/½ cup shelled
* roasted peanuts*
a few fresh coriander
* leaves, chopped*

Preheat the oven to 180°C/350°F/gas 4. Trim the meat and cut it into ribs, if this has not already been done. Salt and pepper the ribs and bake them in the oven for about 1 hour, uncovered.

Meanwhile, prepare the sauce by combining the tomato purée, chilli sauce, *chipotles*, sugar or honey and vinegar in a blender. Do not salt it. Remove the ribs from the pan and raise the heat to 220°C/425°F/gas 7. Coat the ribs thoroughly with sauce and put them back in the oven.

After 20 minutes remove the ribs, transfer them to another bowl and let them stand, while you deglaze the baking juices in the pan with a little water and add any extra sauce. Cook the mixture over low heat, scraping off the bits sticking to the pan. Grind the peanuts coarsely and add them to the sauce. Pour this over the ribs, heat them up again, garnish with coriander and serve.
Serves 4

ITALIAN ROAST SPICED PORK WITH TWO SAUCES

This recipe is equally suitable for wild and domestic pig – it is a good way of
cooking rather tough meat that could not be roasted in the ordinary way.

1.2 kg/2½ lb loin, with
   the bone left in
2 l/3½ pints/9¼ cups
   dry white wine
2 l/3½ pints/9¼ cups
   white wine or cider

vinegar
1 tablespoon chopped
   celery
1 tablespoon chopped
   carrot
1 tablespoon chopped

onion
1 teaspoon juniper
   berries, lightly
   crushed
1 teaspoon rosemary
1 teaspoon tarragon

½ teaspoon ground black
   pepper
2 tablespoons olive oil
salt

Make a marinade for the pork with all the other
ingredients above except the oil and salt. Marinate for 2 days.

Preheat the oven to 150°C/300°F/gas 2. Remove the meat, pat dry and brown well in the
olive oil in a large flameproof casserole. Pour all
the marinade over the meat and add a little salt.
Bring to the boil, transfer to the oven and cook,
uncovered, for 2 hours, turning the meat every
15 minutes. Serve with one of the following
sauces:

SAUCE 1:
250 ml/8 fl oz/1 cup
   beef consommé
2 tablespoons raisins
1 tablespoon pine nuts
1 teaspoon cornflour

juice and grated zest of
   1 lemon
good shake of
   Worcestershire sauce
salt and black pepper

Mix all the ingredients, bring to the boil and
cook for 5 minutes. Pour over the meat and
serve with boiled potatoes.

SAUCE 2:
60 ml/2 fl oz/¼ cup
   cognac
500 ml/16 fl oz/2 cups
   hot béchamel sauce

250 ml/8 fl oz/1 cup
   single cream
½ teaspoon ground
   white pepper
salt, if needed

Warm the cognac, light it and pour into the
béchamel sauce. Stir in the cream and pepper and
heat the sauce without boiling it. Pour over the
meat and serve with a side dish of fried apples.
Serves 4

A wild pig which has
enjoyed a diet
predominately of acorns
and walnuts in the south-
west of France, or north
of Italy, will taste quite
different, even if cooked
the same way, to the
bearded pig of Borneo,
which is hunted in the
forests of Sarawak, and
live on roots, and lives on
roots, herbs and grasses.
The bearded pig provides
nearly half the total
annual protein
requirement for the entire
1.4 million population of
Sarawak.

RAJASTHAN SPICED PRESERVED WILD BOAR

In the absence of wild boar, this can be made with ordinary pork.

1 kg/2 lb boned meat
about 600 ml/1 pint/2½
  cups oil
3 large onions, chopped
12 cloves garlic, crushed

5 cm/2 in fresh ginger,
  crushed
4 teaspoons ground red
  chillis
juice of 2 lemons

120 g/4 fl oz/½ cup
  vinegar
4 teaspoons ground
  cumin
1 tablespoon ground

coriander
1 teaspoon ground cloves
1 teaspoon ground
  cinnamon
4 teaspoons salt

Cut the meat into small cubes. Heat 250 ml/ 8 fl oz/1 cup oil in a frying pan or wok and fry the meat pieces until lightly browned. Remove them and set aside. Add the chopped onions and garlic to the oil and fry until golden. Add the ginger and ground chilli. Cook all these together for 5 minutes more.

Add the lemon juice and vinegar to the pan. Cook for a further 5 minutes, then add the meat and the remaining spices and salt. Cook for a further 10 minutes, then leave to cool. Also heat the remaining oil separately in a saucepan, and let it cool. Sterilize some preserving jars with boiling water.

Put the cooled meat mixture into the dried jars and add enough of the cooled oil to cover it completely. If there is not enough oil, heat some more and let it cool before adding to the meat. Cover the meat and leave it for 2 days in the refrigerator before serving. Remove it from the jars with a wooden spoon.
Serves 4

BEAR

Until they are two years old, bears eat mainly berries and roots. After this age, they become omnivorous, and eat fish and meat, happily raiding dustbins for oddments we consider carrion, or at least unsavoury. If a bear has been eating fish, its flesh will be tinged with this taste, and even marinating and heavy seasoning will not completely mask the fish flavour.

My own culinary experience has not, to date, extended to dealing with bear, but I have found it well recommended in many books. In the United States and Canada bear meat is considered one of the finest game roasts when prepared in the same way as roast pork loin. The excess fat should be trimmed. This is one game meat which is not lacking in fat.

An enthusiastic nineteenth-century hunter in India wrote in his book of experiences that he was curious to see whether bear's haunch could, as people claimed, really be cured to taste like the best York ham. He tried, using a molasses based sweet-cure recipe, and was delighted with the result.

SPICED BEAR

Should you not have a bear handy, make this recipe with lamb. I have tried that and found it excellent.

1.5-2 kg/3-4 lb roasting meat, trimmed of excess fat	page 152)	cinnamon	paste, or crushed fresh ginger
cooked marinade (see	2 tablespoons clear honey	2 teaspoons crushed garlic	salt and black pepper
	1½ teaspoons ground	2 teaspoons ginger	a few sprigs of rosemary
			120 g/4 oz/½ cup butter

Marinate the meat overnight.

Preheat the oven to 240°C/475°F/gas 9. Wipe the meat dry and rub it with a mixture of honey, cinnamon, garlic, ginger, salt and pepper. Stab it all over so that the flavours seep into the meat. Lay the meat on top of some twigs of rosemary, on a big sheet of aluminium foil. Dot it with butter and lay another twig on top, then wrap foil round the meat, several layers thick, turning the edges so that no juices can escape. Cook it in the oven for at least 3 hours.

To remove the meat from the foil, first cut along one of the turned edges and pour off the juices, then cut open the package and slip the meat on to a hot plate with the juices around it. It is a tender and succulent dish, and I don't think you can overcook it. But be warned: the meat will shrink quite considerably during the cooking.

Serves 6

Bear's paws, too, are considered a delicacy, and here is a recipe from *La Gastronomie en Russie*, published in 1860. Skin and wash the bear paws. Marinate them for at least 48 hours, then blanch and refresh them, and simmer with various vegetables and herbs. When they are cooked and tender, drain them put them on a dish, and slice them lengthwise into five sections. Lard them, then brown under a hot grill. Serve them with either a spicy sauce, or a sweet-sour one.

CAPRETTO FARCITO
STUFFED KID

Kid is not normally considered game. But there are plenty of wild goats in many parts of the world, so I make no apologies for including the following heroic recipe. This recipe for kid in Calabria is also delicious roasted out of doors on a charcoal fire.

1 kid, about 8 kg/16 lb	sprig each of fresh	2 bay leaves	800 g/1 lb 10 oz
salt	rosemary, sage,	black pepper	spaghetti
120 g/4 oz/½ cup lard	parsley and basil		250 g/8 oz/1 cup butter

Clean and gut the kid. Take all the edible parts of the entrails, heart, liver and kidney, wash and trim them as necessary, sprinkle with salt and chop finely. Cook these in the lard with rosemary, sage, parsley, basil, bay leaves and pepper. Cook the spaghetti in plenty of boiling salted water until *al dente* (chewy but not soft) and combine with the entrail sauce. Preheat the oven to 230°C/450°F/gas 8.

Butter and salt the whole kid, stuff it with this spaghetti mixture and sew up. Put it in a large roasting pan and sear in the oven for 15 minutes, then turn the oven down to 170°C/325°F/gas 3 and cook for about another 1¼ hours. Baste it often with its own juices.
Serves about 20

SMALL FURRED GAME

RABBIT AND HARE

Wild rabbits are found worldwide, and are often numerous enough to be a pest; yet this was not always so. In classical times they were found only in Spain and the Balearic islands. The Latin name for Spain, *Hispania*, is said to be derived from a Phoenician name meaning 'land of rabbits'. Rabbits were at first a highly prized delicacy, and were farmed for rich men's tables. They were brought to Britain by the Normans.

Wild rabbit is smaller than the tame variety, with darker, gamier meat. The recipes here are mostly for small wild rabbits, but can be adapted to tame rabbit by multiplying the quantities of other ingredients by 1½ or 2. Hare is considerably larger than rabbit, and also dark and gamey.

RUM RABBIT

1 rabbit, about 1.2 kg/
   2½ lb, jointed
500 ml/16 fl oz/2 cups
   dry red wine
1 teaspoon thyme

175 g/6 oz/1 cup stoned
   prunes
120 ml/4 fl oz/½ cup
   dark rum
60 g/2 oz/¼ cup belly

of pork, diced
2 tablespoons oil
flour to dredge
salt and black pepper
2 onions, finely chopped

bouquet garni made
   with parsley, bay
   leaf, celery leaves,
   marjoram and a piece
   of lemon zest

Marinate the rabbit in wine and thyme for 1 day, turning frequently. Soak the prunes in the rum.

Brown the pork in the oil. Remove it with a slotted spoon and set aside. Drain the rabbit pieces, reserving the marinade, dry them and dredge with flour seasoned with salt and pepper. Brown the rabbit in the oil, and set aside.

Cook the chopped onions in the same oil until they are transparent and soft. Add the belly of pork, rabbit and marinade. Then add the prunes and rum and the *bouquet garni*, and simmer, covered, for 2 hours or until tender. Discard the *bouquet garni* and season before serving.
Serves 4

TUDOR RABBIT

We now consider recipes for meat with fruit to be rather exotic, but they were
popular in England in mediæval and Tudor times. Jerusalem artichokes arrived in
Europe from America in the 1570s.

*1 rabbit, about 1.2 kg/
2½ lb, jointed
2 tablespoons of raisins
soaked in a little
white wine
30 g/1 oz/2 tablespoons
butter
1 rasher bacon, chopped*

*a little flour
½ bottle red wine
4 Jerusalem artichokes,
scraped and thickly
sliced
1 large onion, chopped
60 g/2 oz/scant 1 cup
mushrooms, peeled*

*and chopped
1 carrot, chopped
2 apples, peeled, cored
and sliced
½ orange, peeled and
sliced
90 g/3 oz/heaped ½ cup
grapes, seeded and cut*

*in halves
2 cloves of garlic
bouquet garni made
with thyme, parsley
and marjoram
2 bay leaves
strip of lemon zest*

Brown the rabbit pieces in the melted butter and
chopped bacon in a casserole. Sprinkle with a
little flour and add some of the red wine. Add the
rest of the ingredients, cover with a tight-fitting
lid and simmer gently, either in the oven at
170°C/325°F/gas 3 or on top of the stove, for
about 2 hours or until tender.
Serves 4

CONIGLIO CON LE PENNE
RABBIT WITH PASTA

*1 rabbit, about 1.2 kg/
2½ lb, jointed
1 medium onion,
chopped
1 large carrot, chopped*

*1 small bunch of parsley
3 or 4 tablespoons olive
oil
500 g/1 lb/1 lb peeled
tomatoes, chopped (or*

*a 397 g/14 oz tin –
reserve the liquid)
a little stock, if needed
a little tomato juice (or
liquid from tin)*

*salt and black pepper
500 g/1 lb/2¾ cups
penne (short, wide
pasta tubes)*

Reserve the liver and other edible entrails from
the rabbit. Put the onion, carrot and parsley in a
pan with the olive oil. When the onion colours
add the rabbit, allow it to fry lightly, then add
the tomatoes. Cook, covered, over low heat; it
will take 30 minutes to 1 hour. When the rabbit is

half cooked add the liver and entrails, chopped. Moisten with stock if necessary.

When the rabbit is cooked, remove it from the pan and keep warm, then thin the gravy with tomato juice and bring to the boil. Add salt and pepper to taste, then throw in the *penne*, return to the boil and continue cooking briskly.

When the pasta is beginning to soften, replace the rabbit pieces and cook until the pasta is just *al dente* – tender but still slightly resistant. Remove it from the heat at once and serve.
Serves 4

SPANISH RABBIT IN ALMOND SAUCE

1 rabbit, about 1.2 kg/ 2½ lb jointed
salt and black pepper, plus 12 whole peppercorns
60 ml/2 fl oz/¼ cup olive oil
1 onion, chopped
6 cloves garlic, peeled but left whole
25 almonds, blanched and skinned
¼ teaspoon ground cinnamon
1 heaped tablespoon chopped parsley
2 cloves
½ teaspoon saffron
3 bay leaves
250 ml/8 fl oz/1 cup dry white wine

Rub the pieces of rabbit with salt and ground pepper and set them aside. Heat the oil in a pan and cook the onion, 5 cloves of garlic and the almonds, with the rabbit's liver if available, until just browned. Remove to a mortar or blender, and crush with the remaining clove of garlic, cinnamon, parsley, peppercorns, cloves, saffron and salt.

Slowly brown the rabbit pieces in the pan, then add the mortar mixture to the rabbit, throw in the bay leaves and slowly pour in the white wine. Cover, and simmer until the rabbit is very tender, 30 minutes to 1 hour, depending on the rabbit. If more liquid is required, add a little light stock or water.
Serves 4

CONIGLIO RIPIENO CON CARNIOFI
RABBIT STUFFED WITH ARTICHOKES

Rabbit is eaten a great deal in Italy and France. This recipe is from the Maremma, a recently drained marshy area in Tuscany and a hunter's paradise. The wine-tarragon perfume of the dish when it is cooking is not easily forgotten. Only white wine should be drunk with this dish.

1 large rabbit or 2 small ones, about 2 kg/4 lb in all
250 ml/8 fl oz/1 cup wine vinegar
1 lemon

4 small globe artichokes
3 large cloves of garlic, coarsely chopped
120 g/4 oz/¼ lb pancetta (or half belly of pork and half

boiled ham), coarsely chopped, plus 4 long strips of pancetta or belly of pork
salt and black pepper
1 tablespoon fresh

tarragon, or 1½ teaspoons dried
5 tablespoons olive oil
about 600 ml/1 pint/2½ cups dry white wine

Wash the rabbit, discarding the entrails including the liver. Put the rabbit in a large bowl containing 1 l/1¾ pints/4½ cups cold water and the vinegar. Soak for 1 hour to remove the gamey flavour.

Meanwhile, cut the lemon in half and put it in a bowl of cold water. Soak the artichokes in this for 20 minutes, then wash, trim the leaves and cut the artichokes into small pieces, using both body and stems. Place these in a clean bowl. Add the garlic, *pancetta* (or pork and boiled ham) to the bowl with the artichokes. Add salt, pepper and tarragon and mix well. Preheat the oven to 190°C/375°F/gas 5.

When the rabbit has finished soaking wash it in cold running water, ensuring that all the cavities are clean. Dry with paper towels. Stuff the cavity of the stomach with artichoke mixture. Sew it up with a larding needle, then lard each leg with a strip of *pancetta* or pork.

Pour the olive oil into a large baking pan, put the rabbit in this, season, and add enough wine to cover two-thirds of the rabbit. Roast for 1 to 1½ hours, turning twice in this time. Remove the thread before serving. Serve with more artichokes, steamed or braised.
Serves 6.

CONIGLIO IN AGRODOLCE
RABBIT IN SWEET-SOUR SAUCE

*1 large or 2 small
   rabbits, about 1¾kg/
   3½ lb in all, cut into
   12 pieces
500 ml/16 fl oz/2 cups
   dry red wine*

*2 red (or mild white)
   onions
3 bay leaves
6-8 black peppercorns,
   plus salt and ground
   pepper*

*60 ml/2 fl oz/¼ cup
   wine vinegar
120 g/4 oz/scant 1 cup
   flour
5 tablespoons olive oil
60 g/2 oz/⅓ cup raisins*

*1 heaped tablespoon
   light brown sugar
60 g/2 oz/⅓ cup pine
   nuts*

Put the pieces of rabbit in a large bowl. Heat the wine, 1 whole onion, bay leaves, peppercorns, and 1 tablespoon wine vinegar in a saucepan. When the mixture boils, remove it from the heat and pour it over the rabbit. Allow to marinate for 2 hours.

Remove the rabbit pieces and dry them, place them in a large paper bag with the flour, and coat evenly. Strain and reserve the marinade.

Chop the remaining onion coarsely, and put it in a large flameproof casserole with the olive oil. Sauté for 4 to 5 minutes. Add the rabbit and sauté until golden all over, about 15 minutes. Season and continue to cook gently for a further 25 minutes, adding the reserved marinade little by little. Meanwhile, soak the raisins in luke-warm water for 20 minutes to plump them up.

Heat the remaining wine vinegar with the sugar in a small saucepan. When the sugar has dissolved and the mixture is hot, add the drained raisins and the pine nuts and remove from the heat. Cover, and let it stand until needed. Pre-heat oven to 190°C/375°F/gas 5.

When the rabbit has absorbed all the wine and is almost cooked, remove the casserole from the fire. Pour in the contents of the saucepan and stir with a wooden spoon. Cover the casserole and cook it in the oven for a further 15 to 20 minutes. Serve hot.
Serves 6

Whether the manuscript known as the Codex Romanoff is truly the kitchen notes of Leonardo da Vinci, or whether it is a spoof manuscript from the prolific creative pen of Anon, I cannot tell you. However, the version of *Leonardo's Kitchen Note Books*, 'newly rendered into English and edited by Shelagh and Jonathan Routh', is a book I value for amusement and pleasure. Amongst the many endearing grumbles, anecdotes, and words of advice is one complaining about the table manners of Lord Lodovico, who, it seems, tethered 'beribboned rabbits to the chairs of his table guests, that they may wipe their grease-ridden hands upon the beasts' back . . .'.

CONIGLIO IN FRICASSEA
FRICASSÉE OF RABBIT

Rabbit fricassée is a familiar dish. This is a good Italian version with the egg and lemon thickening often used in Middle Eastern cooking.

1 rabbit, about 1.2 kg/	*1 whole)*	*1 stick celery, cut in half*	*2 egg yolks, beaten*
2½ lb	*2 tablespoons olive oil*	*1 medium carrot*	*juice of 1 lemon*
2 medium onions (1	*100 ml/3½ fl oz/⅓ cup*	*sprig of basil*	
finely chopped and	*stock*	*salt and white pepper*	

Cut the rabbit into fairly small pieces. Lightly cook the chopped onion in a deep pan with the olive oil until golden. Add the rabbit and cook over high heat, turning continuously. Add the stock, the remaining onion, celery, carrot and basil tied in a bundle, salt and white pepper. Cover with a lid and simmer for 1½ hours.

Remove the rabbit pieces and arrange on a platter, then, keeping the pan just off the flame, pour the beaten egg yolks and lemon juice into the sauce and leave it to thicken without boiling. Pour the sauce over the rabbit and serve the dish immediately.
Serves 4.

CONIGLIO ALLA CACCIATORA
HUNTER'S RABBIT

Alla Cacciatora is a good way of cooking any small game of dubious age and tenderness. I sometimes add a handful of black olives, pitted and roughly chopped. Serve it with pasta, rice, potatoes or crusty hot bread.

An alternative version, from Lucca, is made in the same way as the previous recipe, but add 200 g/7 oz/1 cup dried black olives at the same time as the tomatoes, and add the liver and kidneys when the olives have softened slightly.

1 rabbit, about 1.2 kg/	*2 cloves of garlic*	*dry white wine*	*salt and black pepper*
2½ lb jointed	*1 sprig of rosemary*	*500 g/1 lb peeled,*	*about 250 ml/8 fl oz/1*
2 tablespoons olive oil	*100 ml/3½ fl oz/⅓ cup*	*seeded tomatoes*	*cup stock*

Reserve the liver and offal of the rabbit.

Heat the olive oil and add the garlic and rosemary. When the garlic is golden put the rabbit in and fry it lightly over a high heat. Add the wine and, after this has evaporated, add the tomatoes,

salt and pepper. Cover with a lid and simmer slowly for 1½ hours or until tender, adding enough stock when necessary to keep it moist and the liver and offal when half cooked.
Serves 4

HARE IN CREAM SAUCE

1 hare, about 3 kg/
   6 lb
2 large carrots, diced
1 small turnip, diced
1 large onion, chopped

100 ml/3½ fl oz/⅓ cup
   wine vinegar
10 black peppercorns
6 bay leaves
4 juniper berries,

   crushed
1 strip of lemon zest
60 g/2 oz/¼ cup butter
salt and ground black
   pepper

3 rashers of bacon
1 tablespoon flour
120 ml/4 fl oz/½ cup
   cream or crème fraîche

Cut the hare into pieces over a basin, taking care that all the blood goes into this. Remove the ribs and abdominal skin. Put the pieces of meat into a basin, and add water to cover. Then pour all these liquids into a saucepan, add the vegetables, vinegar, peppercorns, bay leaves, juniper berries and lemon zest, and slowly bring to the boil. When it has reached a brisk boil, pour it over the hare, cover the basin and leave this in a cool place for at least 1 day, 2 if possible.

Preheat the oven to 200°C/400°F/gas 6. Melt the butter in a large roasting pin, salt the meat and put it in the tin, then cover it with bacon. Roast for 45 minutes, then add as much of the marinade and vegetables as you can fit in the pan. Continue as the liquids evaporate.

When the hare is tender, arrange the meat on a hot dish. Strain the juices into a saucepan, pressing the vegetables through a sieve. Mix some flour to a paste with water, add this to the gravy and cook it to thicken it. Add the cream, adjust the seasoning, and pour it over the hare. Serve with noodles or dumplings, and cranberries.
Serves 6

LEPRE IN AGRODOLCE
HARE IN SWEET-SOUR SAUCE

1 hare, about 3 kg/6 lb, jointed
about 50 ml/1¾ fl oz/ 3⅓ tablespoons vinegar
60 g/2 oz/¼ cup butter

1 large onion, finely chopped
90 g/3 oz pancetta or bacon, chopped
½ teaspoon thyme
1 bay leaf

pinch of ground cinnamon
salt and black pepper
600 ml/1 pint/2½ cups stock
1 tablespoon sugar

60 g/2 oz/⅓ cup seedless raisins
60 g 2 oz/⅓ cup blanched, shredded almonds
2 teaspoons grated unsweetened chocolate

Wash the hare in vinegar, and sauté it in butter with the onion, *pancetta*, sugar, thyme, bay, cinnamon, salt and pepper. Add the stock and simmer slowly until the hare is nearly cooked – it will take 1½ to 2 hours in all.

Dissolve the sugar in vinegar, and stir this into the sauce. Reduce the cooking liquid by simmering without a lid. Add the raisins, almonds and chocolate, and finish cooking.
Serves 6

LEPRE ALL'AGRO
HARE WITH OIL AND LEMON

1 young, tender hare, about 1½ kg/3 lb
120 ml/4 fl oz/½ cup olive oil
juice of 2 lemons

2 tablespoons fresh thyme
4 bay leaves, crumbled
salt and black pepper

60 g/2 oz/½ cup fatty ham, chopped
100 ml/3½ fl oz/3⅓ cup dry red wine

about 100 ml/3½ fl oz/⅓ cup stock, as needed
30 g/1 oz/2 tablespoons butter

Clean the hare, reserving the liver and offal. Marinate the hare, still whole, in 60 ml/2 fl oz/¼ cup oil, the lemon juice, thyme, bay, salt and pepper for some hours, turning frequently.

Put the hare into a pan with the rest of the oil

and ham, fry until lightly browned and add the wine. When the wine has evaporated, leave the hare to continue cooking until tender, adding a little stock now and then. It will take 1 to 1½ hours. Meanwhile, cook the liver and offal in the butter. When cooked, mash them and set aside.

When it is ready, cut it into pieces and put it on a heated serving plate. Thicken the gravy with the mixture of liver and offal, correct the seasoning and pour over the hare.

Serves 4

LEPRE ALLA CACCIATORA
HUNTER'S HARE

1 hare, about 3 kg/ 6 lb, well hung, jointed	1 l/1¾ pint/4½ cups red wine 1 sprig of rosemary	a few sage leaves 2 bay leaves 2 cloves	50 ml/2 fl oz/¼ cup olive oil salt and black pepper

Marinate the hare in the wine with the rosemary, sage, bay leaves and cloves. Leave in this for at least 1 day, turning frequently.

Next day, strain and reserve the marinade. Cook the hare in a pan without adding any seasoning. After the hare has exuded its liquid, add the olive oil, salt and pepper and cook lightly for 10 minutes. Moisten the hare with the reserved marinade, and continue adding slowly as it evaporates. It will take about 1½ to 2 hours in all. Serve very hot with toast or polenta.

Serves 6

LERRNIB
SPICED HARE WITH ONIONS AND SULTANAS

Two of the ingredients for this recipe may be unobtainable. If necessary omit the saffronwood. *Ras el hanoot* is a mixture of about twenty spices, of which the most noticeable ones are cinnamon, cloves, ginger, nutmeg and cardamom. A mixture of these will be a satisfactory substitute. In Morocco, the spice can be bought ready mixed, and is generally used in the cooking of game.

This recipe, the one on page 57, and the tale opposite are included in an enchanting and informative book, *Moorish Recipes*, by John, fourth Marquis of Bute, and I am grateful to the present Marquis for lending me the book and for allowing me to reproduce these recipes.

1 hare, about 3 kg/
*   6 lb, jointed*
3 medium onions,
*   chopped*
salt

1 teaspoon saffron
½ teaspoon ground
*   ginger*
½ teaspoon ground
*   pepper*

2 teaspoons saffronwood
*   (see above)*
1 teaspoon ras el hanoot
*   (see above)*
2 tablespoon chopped
*   fresh parsley*

120 ml/4 fl oz/½ cup
*   olive oil*
1 bunch of spring
*   onions, chopped*
200 g/7 oz/1¼ cups
*   sultanas*

Simmer the hare pieces in a covered casserole with the onions, salt, spices, parsley, olive oil and about 550 ml/18 fl oz/2¼ cups water until the meat is almost tender, about 1½ hours. Add the spring onions and sultanas, simmer for 20 minutes more.

Serves 6

PAPPARDELLE CON LA LEPRE
BROAD NOODLES WITH HARE SAUCE

This is a well-known Tuscan dish. Further details on making pasta are given on page 137.

500 g/1 lb hare meat, chopped or minced
100 g/3½ oz bacon, chopped
1 small onion
1 stick of celery
1 medium carrot

60 g/2 oz/¼ cup butter
30 ml/1 fl oz/2 tablespoons olive oil
2 or 3 cloves
1 tablespoon flour
100 ml/3½ fl oz/⅓ cup dry white wine

500 g/1 lb ripe tomatoes, peeled and chopped
salt and black pepper
grated nutmeg
grated Parmesan cheese, to serve (optional)

NOODLES:
6 eggs
600 g/1¼ lb/4 cups strong flour
1 teaspoon salt
up to 120 ml/4 fl oz/½ cup dry white wine

Begin by making the noodles. Mix 6 eggs with the flour and salt, and knead vigorously, adding just enough white wine to make a very stiff dough. Roll this out very thinly on a floured tabletop – the sheet should be translucent. Lift the sheet off, in several pieces if necessary, and hang it over a broom handle for a few minutes to dry. Return the sheet to the table, cut it into strips about 2.5 cm/1 in wide – use a zigzag cutting wheel if you have one – and hang these up to dry for at least 1 hour.

While the noodles are drying, sauté the bacon, onion, celery and carrots in the oil and butter. Add the hare, cloves, and flour, and continue cooking over a low heat for 15 minutes. Moisten with the white wine, and allow this to evaporate. Add the tomatoes, salt, pepper and nutmeg and cook until well thickened.

Put a very large pan of salted water on to boil, and warm a deep serving dish. When the sauce is ready, throw the noodles into the boiling water and turn the heat right up. By the time the water has returned to the boil, the noodles will have floated to the surface and they will be *al dente* – tender but still slightly chewy. Instantly drain them, tip them into the serving dish, pour on the sauce and serve. In Tuscany grated cheese is not usually served with this dish, but elsewhere most people like this.

Serves 6

This is the last recipe in the Marquess of Bute's *Moorish Recipes*, for *khubz el jarade*, locust bread.

The best way to catch locusts is to repair to the nearest wall, the higher the better. Here, if the season be propitious, numbers of these insects will be found flying with such force against the wall that many will fall senseless to the ground.

Of those that fall, pick up the females – they are easily distinguished from the male in being somewhat larger and rather lighter in colour. Pull off the head as the head is pulled off a shrimp. Then squeeze the body and there will exude the eggs, like dark and diminutive caviare, to the amount of nearly a teaspoonful from each animal. When half a kilo of this spawn has been obtained in a small basin, mix with half a kilo of flour and bake into small loaves.

GAME FISH

SALMON

In *The Tenth Muse*, Sir Harry Luke, then British Chief Commissioner in the Transcaucasian republics of Georgia, Armenia and Azerbaijan, describes eating a species of salmon trout unique to Lake Sevan, and called *Ishkan*, the Prince. It is served surrounded by its own amber-coloured caviare, with an accompanying sauce made of the cream of water-buffalo's milk, mixed with fresh peeled walnuts and a touch of horseradish. This sounds so delectable that even a makeshift version with wild salmon, bought salmon eggs and double Jersey cream is an experiment to be recommended.

I was reminded of this description at a party given by the sculptor Liliane Lijn. A light roulade filled with soured cream and shredded juliennes of smoked salmon was served with freshly grated Parmesan and salmon eggs. A garnish of fresh limes, mmm . . . dream on.

POACHING A SALMON

For a whole fish or a piece of at least 1 kg/2 lb I have been assured that it is possible to cook a salmon by sealing it in foil, placing it in the dishwasher with the plates and cutlery you mean to use (but no washing powder), and parboiled small potatoes (also foil-wrapped) and running the machine. By the time the cycle is finished, they say, the fish and potatoes are cooked, the plates are hot, and everything is ready to go. That may be, I haven't tried it; my dishwasher is deceased and I have not replaced it yet, and even if I had, I doubt if any system is as good as my mother's way of cooking salmon. Overcooking the king of fishes is a sin, it should never be cotton-woolly and pale, but moist, succulent, juicy, its flesh flaking like the petals of some exotic flower. There is no excuse for making a mess of this when it is really so simple to do it correctly.

Butter a large piece of foil. Butter the piece of salmon, then grind fresh sea salt and black pepper over it. Slip a few slices of lemon inside, and a sprig or two of dill, and seal it, folding several layers of foil tightly to ensure that no water seeps in. Place it in a large pan of cold water. An instant before it reaches the bubbling point of boiling, turn the heat off, clap the lid on to the pan and allow the salmon to cool in the water until completely cold. It will continue to cook as it cools. Do not, under any circumstances let the water boil fully.

STEAMED SALMON, WEAVER'S STYLE

tail end of salmon, *boned, and cut* *1 tablespoon butter* *juice of 1 fresh lime or ½*
  about 750 g/ *lengthwise into at* *1 teaspoon fresh dill* *lemon*
  1½ lb, skinned, *least 10 strips* *weed* *salt and black pepper*

Butter a plate or ovenproof dish which will fit easily into your steamer. If you don't have a steamer, use a larger plate to cover a pan of boiling water, and another plate or lid to cover the fish. A steamer is better though, and those pretty Chinese bamboo stacking steamers are inexpensive and are nice enough to be used at the table.

Lay 5 salmon strips side by side, not touching, and interlace the remaining strips to form a weave. Sprinkle with dill, lime or lemon juice, and salt and pepper. Steam for 5 minutes. Serve warm or chilled, with a sauce or with a herb mayonnaise.
Serves 4

STEAMED SALMON WITH FENNEL

Instead of fennel, dill can be used, or a light touch of fresh ginger and lime juice.

750 g/1½ lb boned, *butter* *spinach leaves (or at* *salt and black pepper*
  skinned salmon *1 teaspoon fennel seeds* *a pinch, lettuce),*
1 tablespoon melted *8 large Swiss chard or* *washed*

Cut the fish into 4 portions. Brush each piece with butter, season, and sprinkle with fennel seeds; these have a delicate aniseed aroma. Steam the fish for about 6 minutes. Remove them,

wrap each piece in 2 leaves, and return them to the steamer with the overlapping surface underneath. Steam for a further 2 minutes.
Serves 4

SALMON *ALLA CARBONARA*

This is an adaptation of the well-known recipe for pasta *alla carbonara*. No one knows how it got its name: it is apparently not from the Carbonara restaurant in Rome, nor the nineteenth-century Carbonari who fought for independence, nor the charcoal burners (*carbonair*) after whom that society was named.

225 g/7½ oz fresh salmon (or tinned salmon, or even tuna)
250 g/8 oz/½ lb curly pasta, such as fusilli

(if using fresh pasta, allow 500 g/1 lb
60 g/2 oz/¼ cup butter
2 eggs, beaten

100 g/3½ oz/½ cup freshly grated Parmesan cheese, plus more to serve

60 g/2 oz/1 cup chopped parsley
salt and plenty of black pepper

Drain the fish, if tinned. Break it into large chunks. Set it aside. Cook the pasta until *al dente* – still slightly chewy. Meanwhile, melt the butter. Drain the pasta and quickly return it to the pan, or put it in a very hot serving dish. Immediately pour in the hot butter, tossing to coat the pasta evenly. Add the eggs, Parmesan, parsley, salt and pepper. Toss again, and taste. Sprinkle the salmon chunks over this and toss lightly, taking care not to break up the pieces. Serve with additional grated Parmesan.
Serves 4

SEVICHE
MARINATED SLICES OF SALMON AND MONKFISH

Seviche is raw fish 'cooked' by the action of acid in a marinade of citrus fruit juice and/or vinegar. Prepare the dish the day before, as it needs to stand somewhere cold for a day.

250 g/8 oz/½ lb salmon, boned and skinned

500 g/ 1 lb monkfish, boned and skinned
1 tablespoon sea salt
1 tablespoon caster sugar

juice and grated zest of 3 oranges, plus another orange for garnish

3 tablespoons white wine vinegar
2 green chillies, thinly sliced, seeds removed

Mix the salt and sugar together. Add the orange juice and zest and the vinegar, stir to dissolve the salt and sugar, and add the chillies. Make sure you wash your hands immediately after handling the chillies, and do not touch your eyes or lips during this time. Slice the fish thinly, and leave it in the marinade for 1 day.

Slice the last orange thinly. Drain the fish and arrange it on a dish with the pieces of chilli and zest. Arrange alternate pieces of salmon and monkfish, interspersed with slices of orange.
Serves 4

GRAVADLAX
MARINATED SALMON WITH DILL AND MUSTARD SAUCE

Rondy Kristofferson, who is also my source for the other Scandinavian recipes in this book, taught me this method of making *gravadlax*. You should start at least 3 days before you need the dish.

500 g/1 lb boned fresh salmon
2 tablespoons finely ground sea salt, or to taste
2 tablespoons white

sugar, or to taste
2 teaspoons white peppercorns, crushed, or to taste
100 ml/3½ fl oz/⅓ cup aquavit

small bunch of fresh dill weed
sauce:
handful of fresh dill weed, finely chopped

2 tablespoons mild mustard
2 tablespoons soft brown sugar
1 tablespoon oil

The fish should be in fairly thin slabs to allow the marinade to penetrate. Combine the salt, sugar, peppercorns and aquavit, then rub this well into both sides of the fish. Put half the dill on the bottom of a large dish, lay the fish on top, and cover with the remaining dill. Cover with foil or plastic, put a heavy weight on top and put in the refrigerator to marinate.

After 1 day, turn the fish, baste it with the juices in the dish, cover and weight again. Repeat this process for 3 to 5 days.

Serve with a dill and mustard sauce, made by beating the ingredients together until creamy.
Serves 4-6

Gravadlax is Swedish for buried salmon, but actually it's only marinated. I think I first tasted it at the London restaurant Pomegranates, when it first opened. It used to be a house speciality. Since then it has become a popular restaurant dish, but it is simple to make at home.

CHLOE'S SALMON PASTA

My daughter is an able and imaginative young cook, and has a repertoire of pasta dishes which she makes when inspiration strikes. This might just as easily be in the morning before school, as in the evening on her return. Peas are a favourite ingredient in any of Chloe's pasta dishes, and if there is some leftover salmon . . . well, here's a variation on that theme.

375 g/12 oz/³/4 lb thin spaghetti
120 g/4 oz/¹/2 cup butter
250 ml/8 fl oz/1 cup double cream (or sour cream)
375 g/12 oz/³/4 lb cooked salmon, flaked
250 g/8 oz/1¹/4 cup freshly grated
Parmeson
salt and black pepper
pinch of cayenne pepper
a little freshly grated nutmeg
175 g/6 oz frozen petit pois, thawed
small bunch of flat-leafed parsley, chopped

Cook the spaghetti in plenty of boiling salted water for 5 minutes. Meanwhile, make the sauce. Melt the butter, add the cream, warm it through without boiling, then add the salmon, half the Parmesan, salt, black and cayenne pepper, and nutmeg. When the mixture has warmed up again, throw in the peas and heat everything through – but it must not boil. Pour it over the cooked pasta, sprinkle with parsley and serve with the remaining cheese on the side. *Serves 4*

POACHER'S FISH SOUP

This is a variation on cock-a-leekie. If you add corn kernels, it becomes rather like an American chowder; add fresh kernels at the same time as the milk, or tinned kernels with the fish.

500 g/1 lb skinned and boned salmon (use the skin and bone to make stock)
3 tablespoons butter
2 or 3 leeks, including some of the green, cut into very thin strips
1 large potato, peeled and diced
500 ml/16 fl oz/2 cups fish stock (or light chicken or vegetable stock)
750 ml/1¹/4 pints/3 cups milk
750 ml/1¹/4 pints/ 3 cups double cream
salt and black pepper

Melt the butter in a large pan over a low heat. Add the leeks, and let them soften but not brown. Stir in the potatoes. Pour in the stock, and simmer over a low heat for 15 minutes. Add the milk and cream. Continue simmering the soup for another 10 minutes, but do not allow the soup to boil. Add the salmon and simmer until it is just cooked, about 5 minutes more. Season and serve.

Serves 6

MINIATURE *COULIBIACS*
SALMON PASTIES

Coulibiac is the standard French name for the famous Russian *kulebyaka*, a large and splendid pie usually made with a mixture of fish such as salmon and sturgeon, and *vyaziga* (dried sturgeon's spinal cord). Here is a simplified version lacking that daunting ingredient and made in miniature form to be served as part finger food, picnic food or a starter. It uses *filo* pastry, so the result is rather like Turkish *börek*.

60 g/2 oz/scant 1 cup mushrooms
120 g/4 oz/½ cup butter
375 g/12 oz/¾ lb cooked salmon, flaked
6 spring onions, chopped
120 g/4 oz/⅔ cup cooked rice
1 teaspoon chopped fresh dill weed
salt and black pepper
150 ml/5 fl oz/⅔ cup sour cream, plus more to serve
12 sheets filo pastry (250 g/8 oz/½ lb)
oil for deep frying
lemon slices, to serve

Lightly cook the mushrooms in 1 tablespoon butter until barely softened. Combine these with the salmon, spring onions, rice, dill, salt and pepper, and bind with sour cream to make a filling.

Melt the remaining butter. Cut each sheet of *filo* lengthwise into 4 strips, brush melted butter over each strip, put a spoonful of filling in one corner, and fold at 45° angle over and over, using the whole strip, to make a triangular parcel. Pinch well closed, deep fry in hot oil until lightly brown, and serve hot with slices of lemon and extra soured cream.

Makes 48

Another tasty filling for *coulibiac* is ground game leftovers combined with pumpkin seeds, pine nuts, chopped spring onion, and cooked *kasha* – buckwheat – mushrooms, too, if they are handy. Serve hot with cranberry sauce. Or try leftover pheasant, minced quite fine, mixed with finely chopped almonds, parsley, and a hot egg and stock mixture to bind. Serve hot, sprinkled with cinnamon and a little icing sugar.

SALMON AND PRAWN SOUFFLÉ

In Irish legend a goddess named Boann created the River Boyne and gave it her name. The stream had previously been a well, shaded by nine magic hazel trees. The divine salmon swallowed the magic hazelnuts, and thus became the wisest creature in the world. The Celtic hero Finn McCool, was aided by the Salmon of Wisdom. The salmon has knowledge of other worldly things, useful to a hero, and protects him. Finn honoured the fish by setting its image on his banner, and during the battle the salmon whispered advice in his ear. The Salmon of Wisdom is found on a number of Gallo-Roman altars, and its presence here signifies not only its wisdom but also its power of prophecy.

250 g/8 oz/½ lb salmon, cooked and flaked
175 g/6 oz prawns, shelled and cooked

butter to grease dish small handful of chopped parsley
1 teaspoon fresh dill weed

salt and white pepper dash of Tabasco sauce
30 g/1 oz pot of potted shrimps, with their butter

120 g/4 oz/1⅔ cups mushrooms, sliced
250 ml/8 fl oz/1 cup double cream
2 eggs, separated

Butter a soufflé dish, and preheat the oven to 200°C/400°F/gas 6. Chop the prawns and combine them with the flaked salmon, parsley and dill. Season with salt and pepper and a dash of Tabasco. Gently heat the potted shrimps in their butter, and add the mushrooms. Let these soften slightly. Stir the cream into the salmon mixture, followed by the egg yolks. Beat the whites separately until stiff peaks form. Line the soufflé dish with the shrimp mixture. Gently fold the egg whites into the salmon mixture. Bake for 30 minutes in the oven, or until risen with a nice brown top.
Serves 4-6

SALMON AND SOUR CREAM OMELETTE

6 eggs
salt and black pepper
175 g/6 oz cooked

salmon, flaked
½ tablespoon grated raw onion

75 ml/2½ fl oz/ generous ¼ cup sour cream

30 g/1 oz/2 tablespoons butter

Beat the eggs lightly. Add 1 tablespoon cold water, and season to taste. Fold the salmon and onion into the sour cream and season. Melt the butter in an omelette pan, add the eggs and cook over a medium heat. When they are just about to set, spoon the salmon mixture across the centre of the omelette, cover, and cook for 1 minute to heat through. Then fold the omelette and turn it on to a hot serving dish.
Serves 2-3

FLOTERES
MEDIEVAL SALMON AND CURRANT DUMPLINGS

These are splendid cooked in clear soup, or as a dish on their own.

*120 g/4 oz/scant 1 cup
  flour
1½ teaspoons baking
  powder
½ teaspoon cinnamon*

*½ teaspoon salt
¼ teaspoon crushed
  fennel seed
¼ teaspoon thyme*

*120 ml/4 fl oz/½ cup
  milk, or more if
  needed
2 eggs, well beaten*

*100 g/3½ oz cooked
  salmon, flaked
100 g/3½ oz/⅔ cup
  washed dried currants*

Combine the dry ingredients, then make a batter with the milk. Add the beaten eggs to the batter. Stir in the salmon and currants. Add more milk if the mixture is too dry.

Moisten your fingers, then form the dough into walnut-sized balls. Drop these into briskly boiling salted water or soup. Reduce the heat to a gentle boil, and cover. In 5 to 10 minutes the dumplings will rise to the top of the liquid. Remove them with a slotted spoon and serve warm, or in the case of soup, leave them in and serve everything together.

TROUT

Salmon and trout belong to the salmonidae family, and are found in many waters world-wide. The Atlantic salmon returns to the ocean as a baby smolt, where it feeds and grows, then returns to the river of its origin in order to spawn. The smolts are distinguished from trout by distinctive marks like thumb prints along their sides. Fishermen carefully throw these back if they come on the line.

The sea trout, or salmon trout, is considered to have the best qualities of both salmon and trout. It is distinguished from salmon by the shape of its head, which is less pointed than sal-mon, and by its tail, which is not forked. It does not reach such large sizes as salmon, and its aver-age weight is around 1.8 kg/4 lbs. Its pink flesh is delicately flavoured.

Rainbow trout have been introduced to many waters, including the British, from North America. They are distinguished by a pinkish band runing down the side, and dark spots on the tail as well as the body.

The brown trout is native to British waters. It is browner than the rainbow, and is densely spotted all over except for the tail. Its flesh is a creamy colour, and to my mind there is nothing more delicious than a brown trout fresh out of the river, immediately cooked in a pan of siz-zling butter. There is a way of catching trout by tickling the water along their sides, then rapidly scooping the fish on to the bank. In Scotland this is known as 'guddlin the troot'.

Salmond or trout which have been reared in a fish farm should be identified as such by the fish-monger. The price of wild fish will be higher than that of farmed fish, and this should be re-flected in the superior flavour.

TROUT IN OATMEAL

This is so simple, I hesitate to give it. On the other hand, it is so delicious, that anyone who hasn't tasted trout in oatmeal has been deprived of a real pleasure. Oatmeal is milled in several grades. For this dish, I prefer medium oatmeal.

2 small brown trout per person, or   *1 medium rainbow oatmeal for coating*   *butter for frying a bunch of fresh parsley*   *salt and pepper*

Clean the trout, slit open and remove the back-bone. Season the oatmeal with salt and pepper, then coat the fish. Melt the butter, and when it is bubbling but not brown, put in the trout. Cook on both sides until golden brown.

Remove and keep warm while you fry the parsley to crispness.

Serve immediately.

SMOKED TROUT WITH *KASHA*

4 smoked trout, about
    250 g/8 oz/½ lb each
1 tablespoon olive oil
120 g/4 oz/generous
    1⅔ cups sliced
    mushrooms

175 g/6 oz/scant 1 cup
    kasha buckwheat,
    washed and rinsed
250 ml/8 fl oz/1 cup
    chicken stock
120 g/4 oz/¼ lb

mangetouts, topped
3 or 4 spring onions,
    chopped (or a red or
    mild onion, sliced
    finely)
fresh dill

sprig of parsley
2 bay leaves
150 ml/5 fl oz/⅔ cup
    soured cream
1 tablespoon grated
    horseradish

Take the flesh off the trout and flake it, not too finely. Heat the olive oil, add the mushrooms, and sauté gently. Add the *kasha* and simmer with the stock.

After 15 minutes, the liquid should be absorbed and the *kasha* cooked. Add the mange-touts, trout flesh, spring onions, chopped dill, parsley and bay leaves. Mix well, and as soon as the mangetouts are cooked but still fairly crisp, serve it with a dish of soured cream mixed with horseradish on the side.
Serves 4

SPEYSIDE SALAD

2 smoked trout, about
    250 g/8 oz/½ lb each
8 slices smoked salmon,

about 200 g/7 oz in
    all
3 tablespoons sour cream

1 heaped teaspoon grated
    horseradish
1 teaspoon lemon juice

black pepper
a few sprigs of fresh dill
1 lemon for garnish

Remove the flesh from the trout. Take care to extract all the bones. Mash it with the sour cream, horseradish and lemon juice, and some pepper. Chop a little dill into the mixture.

Spread the slices of smoked salmon flat. If they are big, cut them into better sizes. Put some of the trout mixture at one end of each smoked salmon slice, and roll it up. Arrange the rolls on a serving dish, and decorate with dill and of lemon.
Serves 4

TROUT FILLETS IN LETTUCE WITH VELOUTÉ SAUCE

4 fresh trout, about 375
g/12 oz/³/₄ lb each,
skinned and filleted
(8 fillets in all)
8 large green lettuce
leaves, preferably cos
salt and black pepper
30 g/1 oz/2 tablespoons
butter
150 ml/5 fl oz/²/₃ cup
dry white wine

150 ml/5 fl oz/²/₃ cup
chicken stock
2 tablespoons finely
chopped onion
2 tablespoons finely
chopped mushroom
stalks
juice and zest of ½
lemon
BREADCRUMB
MIXTURE:

120 g/4 oz/2 cups fresh
breadcrumbs
1 teaspoon each of
chopped parsley,
tarragon and chives
juice and grated zest of
½ lemon
SAUCE:
1 tablespoon butter
1 tablespoon flour
600 ml/1 pint/2½ cups

fish stock made from
trout trimmings
salt and black pepper
¼ mild Spanish onion,
finely chopped
250 ml/8 fl oz/1 cup
chicken stock
1 tablespoon tomato
purée
150 ml/5 fl oz/²/₃ cup
double cream

Blanch the lettuce leaves in a large saucepan of boiling salted water for a few seconds to make them flexible. Remove and place in a bowl of cold water until ready to use, then spread them out on a kitchen towel to dry. Make up the breadcrumb mixture. Preheat the oven to 190°C/375°F/gas 5.

Season the trout fillets on both sides with salt and black pepper, and sauté them in sizzling butter on both sides, about 1 minute for each side or until they start to colour. Remove from the pan.

Cut a rectangle from each fillet about 6-7.5 cm/2½-3 in/2½-3 in long; save the remaining parts for later. Place one trout strip on a lettuce leaf, spread it with a quarter of the breadcrumb mixture, top with a second piece of trout and make a packet with 2 lettuce leaves, tucking in the ends so that all holds together neatly without any need for tying or a toothpick. Make the others in the same way.

Make the velouté sauce by melting the butter in the top of a double saucepan. Stir in the flour

and cook for a few minutes to form a pale roux. Add the fish stock, salt and black pepper. Cook, stirring vigorously with a whisk, until well blended. Add the chopped onion, chicken stock and tomato purée, reduce the heat and simmer gently, stirring occasionally and skimming from time to time until the sauce is reduced to half the original quantity. Strain through a fine sieve. Stir in the cream, season and keep warm.

To bake the trout fillets, place the packets in an ovenproof dish side by side without touching. Pour over most of the wine and half the chicken stock and sprinkle with the chopped onion and mushroom stalks. Bake for about 10 minutes, basting a few times, then keep it warm.

Add the trimmings from the fillets to the juices in the baking pan, then the remaining wine, and boil to reduce it until it is almost a glaze. Stir it into the sauce. Taste and adjust seasonings, and heat to serving temperature. Pour the sauce around each fish packet and serve.
Serves 4

STARGAZEY SALMON TROUT

Stargazey refers to the head and tail of the fish which poke out of the pastry, in the same way that smaller fishes do out of the traditional West Country pie. This is an old recipe.

1 salmon trout, 1.25-1.5 kg/2½-3 lb, skinned, but with tail and head left on
750 g/1½ lb puff pastry, thawed if frozen

60 g/2 oz/1 cup fresh breadcrumbs, soaked in boiling milk
bunch of fresh herbs (ideally chives, tarragon, parsley and thyme)
90 g/3 oz/6 tablespoons butter
salt and black pepper
1 teaspoon ground mace
150 ml/5 fl oz/⅔ cup

double cream
1 egg yolk, beaten
120 g/4 oz/¼ lb peeled prawns or shrimps
lemon slices

Roll the pastry very thin, longer than the fish and three times as wide. Leave the pastry to rest while you prepare the stuffing.

Squeeze athe breadcrumbs to get rid of extra milk. Chop the herbs, set a few spoonfuls aside, and mix the rest into the breradcrumbs, followed by 60 g/2 oz/¼ cup butter and the salt, pepper and mace. Beat the stuffing to a creamy consistency, then stuff the cavity of the fish with it. Preheat the oven to 200°C/400°F/gas 6.

Place the fish in the middle of the puff pastry and brush it generously all over with double cream. Dot the reserved herbs all over, and fold the pastry up from the sides, leaving the head and tail exposed. Make the seam into a neat ridge, in imitation of the marking along the side of a fish, and decorate the pastry with 'scales', using the handle of a spoon. The pastry should be firmly sealed where the neck and head emerge.

Brush the pastry with egg yolk and bake the fish in the oven for 20 minutes, which will puff up the pastry and turn it a pale gold. Lower the heat to 180°C/350°F/gas 4 and bake for another 25 minutes. If the pastry shows signs of becoming brown rather than golden, cover it lightly with foil.

While the fish is cooking, sauté the prawns or shrimps briefly in the remaining butter. Serve the fish on a large plate with prawns and lemon slices around it.
Serves 6

OTHER FRESHWATER FISH

The pike is the largest of British freshwater fish. This is probably the reason it used to be considered a noble fish. It has a wicked-looking head with sharp teeth, its flesh tends to be dry, and care must be taken to remove all the many needlelike bones. Nowadays its flesh is used chiefly for quenelles, which are very fine, light, smooth rissoles, tricky to make successfully. They need a rich sauce to set them off to perfection, such as a Sauce Nantua, and well done can be a royal dish indeed. The roe of pike is slightly poisonous and should not be eaten. Pike will eat other fish in their watery territory, and are not averse to a tasty meal of baby duckling.

Carp have a long association with humanity, and at times in history they have been kept as pets, learning to come for feeding when summoned by a bell, and allowing underwater caresses. Izaak Walton called carp the queen of rivers, and they were kept in monastery fish ponds. In China and Japan many types of carp have been bred, and they can live to a great age and size. Nowadays, Israel exports fresh mirror carp to Europe. The flesh absorbs flavours easily, and if you have any doubts it is best to soak the fish for at least 3 hours in salt water before cooking. Carp caught in lakes and sluggish rivers often have a muddy taste and smell unless treated this way. A robust sauce or flavoursome stuffing, and basting well during cooking, to avoid woolliness, achieves a delicious result. Matelot (stew) of eels and carp is a popular dish in the Loire region of France.

BAKED STURGEON OR PIKE

Sturgeons are caught in the Black Sea and Caspian, in northern waters, in some parts of the United States, and occasionally off the coast of Scotland. This recipe can also be made with pike, shark, swordfish or other close-textured fish.

900 g/2 lb fish	*2 glasses dry white wine*	*1 dessertspoon flour*	*1 teaspoon chopped fresh*
salt and freshly ground	*30 g/1 oz/2 tablespoons*	*600 ml/1 pint/2½ cups*	*dill weed*
pepper	*butter*	*single cream*	*grated nutmeg*

To remove the skin, either scald the fish several times, or marinate it for several hours, or stand it in salt and water for several hours, after which time the skin can be removed more easily. I prefer the scalding method.

An hour before the fish is required, preheat the oven to 200°C/400°F/gas 6, rub the fish all over with salt and lay it in an ovenproof dish. Pour the wine over, then put it in the oven.

Make a roux with the butter and flour, then gradually add the cream, stirring constantly. Season, add the chopped dill, nutmeg, and pour some of the sauce over the fish. Occasionally add more sauce to the fish, until it becomes a golden brown and forms a light crust. When the fish is tender and flakes easily serve it with steamed potatoes, or sprinkled with more chopped dill. *Serves 4-6*

MOUSSELINE OF PIKE WITH CRAB

500 g/1 lb pike fillets,
   skinned
3 large egg whites
salt
cayenne pepper
paprika
450 ml/15 fl oz/scant 2
   cups double cream

about 250 g/8 oz/2
   cups crab meat, from
   2 small or 1 large crab
   (if using frozen crab
   meat, allow an extra
   120 g/4 oz/1 cup for
   sauce)
1 medium onion,
   chopped

6 shallots, chopped
1 small leek, chopped
3 tomatoes, chopped
2 stalks of celery,
   chopped
1 medium carrot,
   chopped
small sprig of fresh
   tarragon

1 bay leaf
100 ml/3½ fl oz/⅓ cup
   white wine
60 g/2 oz/¼ cup
   unsalted butter
a little sherry vinegar or
   lemon juice

Preheat the oven to 180°C/350°F/gas 4. Empty the crab shell and reserve the meat. Roast the shell in the oven for 15 minutes with the chopped vegetables, tarragon and bay leaf. Add the wine to the pan, put it on the oven, bring back to the boil and stir, scraping up the residue sticking to the pan sides and bottom. (If you are using frozen crab, omit this step, and carry out the next step with 120 g/4 oz/1 cup crab, the vegetables, herbs and wine.)

Transfer the mixture to a clean pan, add about 500 ml/16 fl oz/2 cups water and simmer with the lid on for 2 hours.

Beat the fish and egg whites to a smooth purée, season with salt, cayenne and paprika and sieve. Place this in a bowl in a bed of crushed ice. Beat the mixture vigorously, gradually adding 300 ml/10 fl oz/1¼ cups of the cream. Continue beating until the mixture is well aerated. Test for seasoning and consistency by poaching a tablespoon in simmering water for 5 minutes. It should hold its shape and be light and fluffy. Adjust it if necessary with more fish or more cream. Reserve the mousseline in the refrigera-

tor while you prepare the crab sauce.

Strain the stock, discarding the pieces of shell. Return to the pan, add the remaining cream and bring it back to the boil. Reduce as much as necessary to obtain a smooth consistency, and finish by whisking in 30 g/1 oz/2 tablespoons cold butter. Adjust the seasoning with vinegar or lemon juice to taste. Keep the sauce warm. Preheat the oven again to 180°C/350°F/gas 4.

Use the remaining butter to grease 6 dariole moulds (not too small) and 6 pieces of foil to cover them. Spoon some of the mousseline mixture into the moulds, filling each about one-third full and leaving a hollow in the centre. Fill this with crab meat and cover with more mousseline, but do not fill the moulds right to the top. Smooth out the surface of the mixture and cover each mould with foil. Stand the moulds in a roasting pan three-quarters immersed in boiling water and cook in the oven for about 20 minutes, or until the mixture has risen. Turn out and coat with the sauce. Serve at once.

Serves 6 as a starter

REGINA IN PORCHETTA
'QUEEN' CARP BAKED LIKE SUCKLING PIG

In Perugina, the carp from nearby Lake Trasimeno is called *regina*, both for its size
and for its exquisite flavour. This recipe is adapted to a carp of ordinary size.

An engraving of
Careme's piece *montee* for
a fishing party shows an
extraordinary concoction.
A column 1.2-1.5 m/4-5
ft/4-5 ft high rose from a
mass of foliage, made
from leaves of mashed
and tinted potato piped
into extraordinary forms.
The column was
garlanded with pale full-
blown flowers of lobster
meat, double-petalled.
Surmounting the column
was a pedestal, edged
with shrimp 'rosebuds'
and shells, containing a
crystallized blue-green
sugar pool, and out of
this emerged a plump fish
holding with one fin a
spun sugar umbrella. The
engraving is headed 'A
Culinary Fantasy, the
Cautious Carp'.

1 carp, about 1 kg/2 lb
150 g/5 oz/⅔ cup lard,
*   diced*

1 clove of garlic,
*   chopped*
salt and white pepper

sprig of herb fennel
1 large sprig of rosemary
50 ml/2¾ fl oz/3⅓

tablespoons olive oil

Preheat the oven to 180°C/350°F/gas 4. Mix the
lard, garlic, salt, pepper and fennel. Stuff the
cleaned fish with some of this, then make several
cuts on the surface of the fish and fill them with
the remaining mixture. Lay the rosemary on the
fish and tie string around it to hold in the stuffing. Put it in a roasting pan, pour on the olive oil
and bake the fish for about 45 minutes.
Serves 4

ITALIAN STUFFED BAKED FISH

This recipe is from Giuseppe Bellini. The vegetable stuffing makes a change from
usual fillings such as breadcrumbs. Use any firm-fleshed white fish of sufficient size.

1 fish, about 1.2 kg/
*   2½ lb*
2 medium onions, sliced
2 medium tomatoes,

sliced
2 medium green
*   peppers, sliced*
salt and white pepper

120 g/4 oz/½ cup butter
1 teaspoon chopped fresh
*   rosemary*
1 teaspoon chopped fresh

thyme
4 rashers bacon
100 ml/3½ fl oz/⅓ cup
*   white wine*

Preheat the oven to 180°C/350°F/gas 4. Clean
the fish. Pack the cavity with half the sliced
vegetables, salt, pepper and a small piece of the
butter. Close up the fish with toothpicks or
small skewers. Lay a sheet of aluminium foil at
the bottom of a roasting pan and butter it. Put
your fish on it. Rub the skin with butter. Season
it with salt, pepper, rosemary and thyme. Lay
the slices of bacon over the top.

Arrange the remaining slices of onion, tomato
and pepper around the fish. Bake, covered, in
the oven for about 30 minutes, basting from
time to time with the melted butter from the
dish, and the white wine.
Serves 4-5

SEAWATER FISH

The only sea fishing I have done is intensely amateur, in a little boat off the point at Buckie, in Banffshire, to catch mackerel with a line. We would go out in the early evening and eat our catch a few hours later, cleaned and grilled, served with a tangy mustard sauce. A far cry from the game-fishing for the great sailfish, swordfish, and sharks. The taste and texture of shark and swordfish are quite similar. The most delicious shark I have tasted is Mako shark, grilled rare. Mako shark, porkeagle shark and white shark are warm-blooded creatures, and their young are born alive. If you find dolphin on an American menu, it is almost certain to be dorado (mahimahi), a salt-water fish, not the cetecean (whale family). There are a number of types of tuna, which include albacore, yellowfin, bluefin, bonito. These are fished in many waters, on the line and also with nets.

Ordinary fishmongers sell several kinds of shark under different names intended to reassure easily frightened buyers: huss, rock salmon and rock eel are the most usual, and sometimes you can find whole small lemon sharks. The well known monkfish is also a kind of shark. Shark, unlike other fish, is improved by not being quite fresh – it is best about 2 days after catching. During this time its unpleasant ammoniacal smell dissipates. It will still smell of ammonia during cooking, but don't worry – by the time it is done it will have quite a delicate flavour.

SWEET-SOUR SHARK

This recipe is not intended only for sea fishermen who have caught a full-sized shark.

1 slice of shark per person, about 250 g/ 8 oz/½ lb each	flour to coat 4 tablespoons olive oil 2 medium onions, sliced	1 tablespoon sugar 50 ml/1¾ fl oz/3⅓ tablespoons white	wine vinegar salt and white pepper

Coat the slices with flour and fry them in half the oil. Drain and transfer to a warm dish. Fry the sliced onions in fresh oil, and when they are golden add the fish. Sprinkle it with the sugar and vinegar, and salt and pepper to taste. Leave it to cool in the sauce, and serve cold.

Serves 4

SWORDFISH IN RED WINE WITH CHERRIES

1.25 kg/2½ lb swordfish
  (or any other firm
  white fish)
600 ml/1 pint/2½ cups
  milk

90 g/3 oz/heaped ½ cup
  sour cherries, stoned
  (weight without
  stones)
1 tablespoon butter

500 ml/16 fl oz/2 cups
  stock or water
1 tablespoon sugar
2 cloves, crushed
pinch of ground

cinnamon
1 teaspoon cornflour
100 ml/3½ fl oz/⅓ cup
  red wine
salt and white pepper

Wash the fish and simmer it, in enough milk to just cover it, for about 10 minutes – do not over-cook. Pour off the milk, scald the fish with boiling water to wash off the milk, dry it and keep it hot. Cook the cherries with just enough water to prevent sticking, rub through a sieve, and cook gently with the butter for 10 minutes or so.

Dilute with stock or water, add the sugar, cloves and cinnamon, and the cornflour mixed to a smooth paste with a little cold water. Bring this to boiling point, add the wine, and simmer for 1 minute. Season with salt and pepper, pour over the fish and serve.
Serves 6

SWORDFISH COOKED IN A *BAIN-MARIE*

4 slices of swordfish,
  about 250 g/8 oz/
  ½ lb each

2 tablespoons chopped
  fresh parsley
1 teaspoon marjoram

1 teaspoon capers
salt and white pepper
2 tablespoons oil

juice of 1 lemon

Choose a round dish or bowl large enough to take the slices in one layer, but small enough to fit inside a large saucepan. Put a rack inside the saucepan and pour in enough water to come just over the top of the rack. Put this on to boil.

Lay the slices in the dish and sprinkle them

with chopped parsley, marjoram, capers, salt, pepper, oil and lemon, and put the bowl in the pan. Cover, and simmer for 10 minutes – do not overcook. Serve the fish with steamed potatoes and a chilled dry white wine.
Serves 4

FRESH TUNA WITH LETTUCE

This recipe is equally good for salmon and swordfish.

4 tuna steaks, about 4
   cm/1½ in/1½ in
   thick, total weight
   about 1 kg/2 lb
4 anchovy fillets
a little milk

juice of 2 lemons
2 tablespoons olive oil
1 medium onion, finely
   chopped
90 g/3 oz/¾ cup celery,
   finely chopped

8 large lettuce leaves
1 tablespoon chopped
   fresh dill weed
1 tablespoon chopped
   fresh parsley
salt and white pepper

2 tablespoons butter
375 ml/12 fl oz/1½
   cups dry white wine

Put the anchovy fillets to soak in milk to remove some of the salt. Bring water to boiling point in a pan large enough to hold the fish steaks. Add the lemon juice to the water. Put in the fish and simmer for a minute.

Meanwhile, take a clean pan and put the oil, onion and celery in layer on the bottom of the pan, and start to cook these. As the onion starts to soften, drain the fish which has just simmered and arrange it on top of these vegetables. Briefly blanch the lettuce leaves in boiling water, and drain and chop the anchovies. Turn the fish over and sprinkle with the anchovies and chopped herbs, salt and pepper. Cover for less than a minute. Remove the fish from the pan, and wrap each piece in two lettuce leaves. Replace in the pan, cover, and cook very gently, gradually adding the butter and wine, for 15 minutes or less. Serve it with the vegetables.
Serves 4

FRESH TUNA WITH PEAS

This recipe is from Italy, where fresh tuna is highly esteemed.

1 kg/2 lb fresh tuna (or
  any firm-fleshed fish)
2 cloves of garlic,
  roughly crushed
120 ml/4 oz/½ cup

olive oil
1 teaspoon salt
½ teaspoon black pepper
2 tablespoon tomato
  purée, diluted in

250 ml/8 fl oz/
  1 cup water
small bunch of parsley,
  coarsely chopped
2 bay leaves

375 g/12 oz/3½ cups
  fresh peas (weight
  without pods)

Cut the tuna into 2.5 cm/1 in/1 in slices. Brown the cloves of garlic in the oil, then discard them. Sauté the fish for 2 minutes on each side in the oil, and add the salt and pepper. Turn the slices again, add the diluted tomato purée, parsley and bay leaves, and simmer for about 5 minutes.

When the slices are cooked, take them out, add the peas, and cook them in the sauce for about 10 minutes. Add more water if the sauce becomes too thick. When the peas are cooked replace the fish, warm it through and serve immediately.
Serves 4

JAPANESE GRILLED FISH FILLETS

The glaze of egg yolks and rice wine makes a delicious coating. You can use dry sherry instead of rice wine. Any firm white fish will do.

8 fish fillets, total
  weight 1 kg/2 lb

sea salt
2 egg yolks

1 tablespoon rice wine
  (or dry sherry)

black pepper
cayenne pepper

Rub a little ground sea salt into the fish fillets and leave them for 10 minutes. Beat the egg yolks with the wine, and season with black and cayenne peppers. Arrange the fish pieces in an ovenproof dish and brush them with half the egg

mixture. Grill them under a medium heat for 5 minutes, turn, brush with the remaining mixture and grill for a further 5 minutes or until cooked.
Serves 4

FISH GALANTINE WITH *SALSA ALLA VICENZINA*

This is an eighteenth-century Italian recipe. It can be prepared well in advance, and is especially suitable for dining on a terrace when you would like something special that offers no last-minute problems in serving. Use any firm-fleshed fish of the right size.

1 whole fish, about 1½ kg/3 lb
600 ml/1 pint/2½ cups dry white wine
4 bay leaves
several sprigs of parsley
leaves from a bunch of celery
several sprigs of herb fennel

zest of 1 lemon
120 g/4 oz/⅔ cup pistachio nuts, shelled
10 g/⅓ oz powdered gelatine
STUFFING:
1 fillet of sole, about 120 g/4 oz/¼ lb pounded

1 small tin (99 g/ 3½ oz) of tuna in oil, pounded
2 eggs
herbs: thyme, marjoram, dill weed etc., to taste
SAUCE:
1 tablespoon capers
2 cloves garlic

1 small truffle
a few sprigs of parsley
a few leaves of basil
100 ml/3½ fl oz/⅓ cup court bouillon from cooking the fish
100 ml/3½ fl oz/⅓ cup dry white wine
juice of 1 lemon

Clean the fish and marinate it for at least 12 hours in the wine with the bay leaves, parsley, celery, fennel leaves and lemon peel. Use the head and trimmings of the fish to make at least 1 1/1¾ pints/4 ½ cups of court bouillon – that is, rather weak fish stock.

Prepare a stuffing made from pounded fillet of sole, tuna in oil, eggs and chopped herbs. Fill the boned and marinated fish with this, make little cuts in the skin, and insert the shelled pistachio nuts. Wrap the fish in muslin and simmer it for 1 hour in the wine marinade mixed with most of the court bouillon (strain these, and carefully skim the court bouillon before using it).

While the fish is cooking, make the sauce. Pound together the capers, garlic, truffle, parsley and basil, and boil these in a little quantity of court bouillon with the wine, lemon juice and vinegar. When it is slightly reduced, add the pepper and olive oil. Leave to cool.

When the fish is cooked, add the gelatine to the liquid and let the fish cool in the liquid. This should set to an aspic.

Remove and unwrap the fish and serve it with the aspic chopped into cubes, and the sauce.
Serves 6

PILÂKI
COLD FISH STEW

Here is a Turkish recipe for cooking any firm-fleshed fish. Tuna, swordfish or shark are all suitable.

In the 1960s I spent about two years living in Turkey and travelling back and forth. Turkish cuisine is imaginative and varied. If anyone tries to tell you it is the same as Greek, then you will know that that person doesn't know what he is talking about. The dishes may be simple or unbelievably elaborate and strange. For instance, when I was eating a delicious pudding and asked what it was made from, I was told something I could not believe, that it was made from pounded chicken breast. I have since discovered a variation of this dish in India, and in fact the origin of the humble British blancmange is in a medieval recipe for a rich sweet dish made with pounded chicken breast and almonds.

750 g/1½ lb fish
2 onions, chopped
5 cloves of garlic,
  crushed

2 tablespoons olive oil
3 medium potatoes,
  peeled and sliced
2 sticks celery, or

120 g/4 oz/1 cup
  celeriac, chopped
2 carrots, sliced
2 large tomatoes, sliced

salt and black pepper
juice of 1 lemon
handful of chopped fresh
  parsley to garnish

Slightly brown the onions and garlic with 1 tablespoon olive oil. Add 250 ml/8 fl oz/1 cup water, let them simmer for a few minutes, and when they are soft mash or sieve them.

Arrange all the other vegetables in an oven-proof dish, pour the puréed onions over this, cover, and cook over medium heat (or in the oven at 180°C/350°F/gas 4) for about 20 minutes, adding more water if necessary. Add the fish cut into slices, season, and pour in the remaining olive oil. Cover, and cook for a further 15 minutes.

Remove the dish from the heat, add the lemon juice and chopped parsley, and leave to cool. Serve cold.

Serves 4

FISH WITH KERALA SAUCE

Kerala state is in the far south of India. Coconut plays an important part in the cooking of the region.

1 kg/2 lb firm white fish
100 ml/3½ fl oz/⅓ cup
  oil
2 large onions, finely
  chopped
2 teaspoons chopped
  garlic

1½ tablespoons chopped
  fresh root ginger
¼ teaspoon ground
  turmeric (I prefer the
  grated zest and juice
  of 1 lime)

2 green chillies (or more
  to taste), seeded and
  chopped
2 tablespoons ground
  coriander

750 ml/1¼ pints/3 cups
  coconut milk (see
  below)
1½ teaspoons coarse salt
2 tablespoons chopped
  fresh coriander leaves

Coconut milk is not the same as the tasteless clear liquid found inside a ripe coconut. You can make it by mixing the shredded meat of 3 coconuts with 750 ml/1¼ pints/3 cups of milk, bringing this to the boil, removing from the heat and leaving for 30 minutes, then straining the mixture through muslin. An easier way is to use 250 g/8 oz/½ lb of desiccated or creamed coconut. A few delicatessens sell coconut milk in tins.

Heat the oil in a large heavy-bottomed pan and add the onion. Fry it over a high heat until golden brown, about 10 minutes, stirring constantly to prevent burning. Reduce the heat to medium, then add the garlic, ginger, turmeric (or lime), chillies, and ground coriander; stir rapidly for 15 seconds, then add the coconut milk and salt. Cook the sauce, uncovered, until it thickens, about 10 minutes, stirring continuously to ensure that the sauce does not stick and burn.

Add the fish, mix, reduce the heat to medium low, and simmer, covered, for 5 to 7 minutes or until the fish is cooked through. Do not overcook. Check the seasoning, stir in the coriander leaves and serve.

Serves 4

ACCOMPANIMENTS

SAUTÉED POLENTA SQUARES

Polenta – coarsely ground maize meal – is a staple food in southern Italy. Like its American equivalent hominy grits in the southern United States, it has little flavour of its own, but is a fine vehicle for other flavours. These squares make a welcome change from potatoes or rice.

350 g/12 oz/2¼ cups polenta
1 tablespoon salt, plus more salt and black
pepper for seasoning
120 g/4 oz/½ cup butter, plus more to grease greaseproof
paper
60 g/2 oz/½ cup freshly grated Parmesan cheese
60 g/2 oz/¼ cup goose fat (or bacon or other fat)

Boil 2½ l/4 pints/2½ quarts water with a tablespoon of salt in a large, heavy pan. Sprinkle the polenta over this, stirring constantly with a wooden spoon. Add 120 g/4 oz/½ cup butter, cut into pieces, and the grated Parmesan. Cook this mixture over a low heat, stirring frequently, for 25 minutes.

Rinse out a wide, shallow ovenproof dish with cold water, and pour in the polenta, spreading it 1 cm/½ in thick with a spatula. Cover the polenta with a buttered sheet of greaseproof paper and let it cool, then chill it until ready to use.

Cut the polenta into 5 cm/2 in squares or diamonds. Heat the fat in a pan and sauté as many at a time as possible over moderately high heat, so that they are lightly browned. Serve these hot with any robust game dish.
Serves 4-6

NARANJI PULAO
ORANGE RICE

This unusual Afghan rice dish is well worth trying as an accompaniment to all sorts of meat and bird dishes. A similar dish is made in Iran, where they call it *shirin polo*, sweet rice.

500 g/1 lb/2⅔ cups basmati rice
shaved peel of 3 oranges (see below)
175 g/6 oz/¾ cup butter
4 medium carrots, cut into thin slivers
90 g/3 oz/½ cup blanched, slivered almonds
90 g/3 oz/½ cup pine nuts
120 g/4 oz/⅗ cup sugar
½ teaspoon saffron, dissolved in a little warm water
90 g/3 oz/½ cup unsalted, shelled pistachios, a few of these coarsely grated
juice of ½ lemon
1 bay leaf
salt and black pepper

Wash the rice well and soak for at least 1 hour.

Peel the rind from the oranges, as thinly as possible – try not to include any white pith. Blanch the rind in boiling water, refresh it in iced water, then cut it into long, thin slivers. I sometimes use scissors for this job in preference to a knife. Melt 60 g/2 oz/¼ cup butter in a heavy pan. Add the carrot slivers and cook them gently without browning. Add the orange rind, almonds, pine nuts, sugar and saffron, and reduce the heat. Stir constantly until the sugar dissolves, then simmer for 15 minutes. Add the whole pistachios and set aside.

Melt the rest of the butter in the bottom of a large, heavy pan, drain the rice and add this to the pan. Mix well with the melted butter, then stir in the lemon juice and drop in the bay leaf. Add hot water, so that it covers the top of the rice by about 2 cm/¾ in/¾ in. If the rice has been really well soaked, just over 1 cm/about ½ in/about ½ in should be sufficient. Mix again, then cover. Bring it to the boil and lower the heat to a slow simmer. You should not need to drain this rice, as the moisture will be absorbed. It will cook in about 15 minutes.

Colour 1 heaped tablespoonful of cooked rice in the saffron mixture, set this rice aside and stir the saffron mixture into the rest of the rice. Season to taste. Turn this rice on to a serving dish, top it with the reserved rice and decorate with the grated pistachios.
Serves 6

I first tasted *naranji pulao* when I was in Afghanistan on a carpet-buying trip. The occasion was a picnic in the hills above Kabul, at the summer villa belonging to Nawroz, a major exporter of antique and new carpets.

His house was built on a steep slope which had been dug out to allow a garden and shaded pool at the back.

There were many courses to this picnic, and *naranji pulao* was heaped high over a variety of roast and steamed birds, a saffron peak atop a rice pyramid. We scooped this out of our large, rose-painted Chinese bowls with pieces of bread torn off huge thin flaps like elephants' ears. The food I ate in Afghanistan was always delicious, the dishes delicate, more akin to Persian, Mogul or Kashmiri food than the spicier taste of Pakistan and India.

NABIL'S CHRISTMAS RICE

Nabil is Sotheby's Islamic manuscript expert, a great cook and generous host. One year he invited me for Christmas lunch, and the traditional turkey was served with this dish as its stuffing and accompaniment. Leftover rice makes a splendid stuffing for peppers, courgettes, tomatoes, cabbage leaves, vine leaves, so make plenty to ensure that you do have leftovers.

500 g/1 lb/2⅔ cups basmati rice (or wild rice), cooked (uncooked weight)
250 g/8 oz/½ lb minced

lamb
120 g/4 oz/⅔ cup pine nuts
120 g/4 oz/⅔ cup blanched, chopped

almonds
60 g/2 oz/¼ cup butter
a little stock or water, if needed
75 g/2½ oz/½ cup

seedless raisins
1 scant teaspoon ground cinnamon
salt and black pepper

Fry the meat and nuts separately in butter. The nuts need very little time to cook; make sure they don't burn. Cook the meat longer, crushing it and breaking up any lumps, until it is evenly browned. You may need to add a little stock or water.

Mix the nuts and meat with the raisins, and stir in the cinnamon, salt and pepper. Combine this mixture with the cooked rice.
Serves 6

CELERIAC GAME CHIPS

500 g/1 lb celeriac serves at least four.
Celeriac crisps make a pleasant version of game chips. Parsnips and large Jerusalem artichokes can be treated in the same way.

1 head of celeriac, as large as needed

juice of 1 lemon, or 2 tablespoons vinegar

oil for deep frying
salt

Peel this ugly-looking vegetable, cut it into long blocks about 4 cm/1½ in thick, and slice these across as thinly as possible. Drop the slices into a bowl of cold water acidulated with the lemon juice or vinegar.

Heat the oil very hot – 202°C/395°F on a cooking thermometer. Drain the celeriac and dry it very thoroughly. Deep fry the slices in batches until they turn golden. Drain them on kitchen paper, sprinkle with salt and serve hot.

RAINBOW RIBBONS

These ribbons are home-made pasta, given different colours and textures by incorporating spices in the dough. Paprika makes an orangey red, turmeric gives yellow, cumin seeds gives an effect reminiscent of an owl's breast feathers, poppy seeds give a speckled blue-black, and so on. Although simple in essence, this is an economical way of making a dramatic party dish which can be served in all sorts of ways, using different sauces and accompaniments. You can add further variety by colouring some of the pasta green with a little spinach purée. The same technique can be used to flavour and colour bread dough.

300 g/10 oz/2 cups wholemeal flour	*3 large eggs, at room temperature*	*¼ teaspoon paprika*	*cumin or coriander seeds (but not a*
1 teaspoon salt	*½ tablespoon olive oil*	*¼ teaspoon turmeric*	*mixture)*
		1 tablespoon poppy,	

Heap the flour and salt in a mound in the middle of a large bowl – as spacious as you can find, to allow yourself lots of working space inside. Make a well in the centre of the flour, and add the eggs and oil. Stir these together, then start to incorporate the flour. When most of the flour has been absorbed, place the dough on a flat surface, sprinkle it with a little flour, and knead for at least 10 minutes working all the flour in. The dough should be smooth-textured but very stiff – if necessary add more flour or a very little water. Return the dough to the bowl, cover with a plastic bag and leave to rest for anything between 30 minutes and 3 hours.

Divide the dough into three portions, and incorporate paprika into one, turmeric into another, and the seeds into the third. If you have a pasta machine, use it. Otherwise, continue to knead each ball of dough until everything is well and truly incorporated. Roll each ball out on a floured tabletop until it is about 1½ mm/¹⁄₁₆ in thick – if it is thin enough it will be translucent. Let these thin sheets rest, covered with a dry tea cloth, for 10 to 15 minutes.

Set a clean broom handle or bamboo pole between two chair backs. Then cut the pasta into ribbons, as wide or narrow as you wish, and hang them over the pole. Don't let them overlap. Leave them to dry for at least 1 hour.

When the pasta is dry but still flexible you can cook it at once, or store it loosely bundled into a plastic container – it will keep in the refrigerator for 2 days or so. It can also be frozen. Cook it (if frozen, without thawing) in a very large pan of fast boiling salted water. It will cook very quickly – if freshly made, by the time the water returns to the boil. It is ready when it floats to the surface. Drain it at *once*, as it will overcook in seconds.

Makes enough for 3 people with sauce.

GAME CHIP BASKETS

Allow 1 medium potato per small basket.
These decorative – and deliciously edible – containers can be used to hold
cranberry sauce, or extra stuffing, or a mixture of chestnuts and pine nuts, or
anything you like. Incidentally, game chips are called that not because they are
made with game but because they are served with it. You might call them potato
crisps with delusions of grandeur. To make the baskets you will need a pair of
wire sieves or small wire baskets which can be fitted closely into each other.

potatoes   *oil for deep frying*   *salt*

Peel the potatoes and slice them very finely on a *mandoline*, or with a sharp knife. Allow them to soak in cold water for 30 minutes.

Dry the slices thoroughly. Heat the oil very hot – if you have a cooking thermometer it should register 202°C/395°F. Dip one sieve or basket into the hot oil, remove it and line the bottom of the basket with overlapping potato slices. Dip the other basket and push it into place on top of these to hold the shape, then plunge it all into hot oil. Deep-fry until crisp and golden. Make as many as you need, drain them on kitchen paper, sprinkle with salt, and keep hot in a low oven.

COURGETTES WITH PINE NUTS

500 g/1 lb courgettes
90-120 g/3-4 oz/½-⅔
cup pine nuts

1 teaspoon Meaux
mustard
juice of ½ lemon

375 ml/12 fl oz/1½
cups buttermilk

a little ground mace or
nutmeg
salt and black pepper

Preheat the oven to 170°C/325°F/gas 3. Wash and dry the courgettes. Cut them into slices about 5mm/¼ in thick. Blanch them briefly in boiling water, but remove them while they are still crisp and drain them. At the same time roast the pine nuts on a baking tray in the oven for about 15 minutes.

Arrange the courgettes in a flat dish. Mix together the mustard, lemon juice, buttermilk, mace or nutmeg, salt and pepper. Sprinkle the pine nuts over the courgettes, add the seasoned buttermilk, and leave to marinate in a cool place for several hours before serving.
Serves 4-6

GLAZED APPLES WITH STUFFED PRUNES

These make a delectable accompaniment to roast goose, or any other roast game.

8 large prunes
about 100 ml/3½ fl oz/
  ⅓ cup port

380 g/12½ oz/1¾ cups
  sugar
4 large, firm red apples

juice of ½ lemon
3 tablespoons cooked,
  mashed goose liver

(may be tinned)
about 1 tablespoon
  double cream

Put the prunes in a saucepan with 75 ml/2½ fl oz/¼ cup port and 2 teaspoons sugar. Let the mixture stand for at least 4 hours, or overnight (if the prunes are of the ready-to-eat stoned prunes, this step is not necessary).

Bring the liquid to the boil and poach the prunes for 10 minutes, then allow them to cool in the liquid, drain them in a colander and if necessary stone them neatly.

Meanwhile, peel and halve the apples, and neatly remove the cores to leave rounded hollows. Boil a mixture of 1 l/1¾ pints/4½ cups water, 380 g/12½ oz/1¾ cups sugar and the lemon juice. Poach the apple halves over moder-ate heat, turning them after about 5 minutes. Preheat the oven to 190°C/375°F/gas 5.

When the apples are tender, take them out with a slotted spoon and arrange them cut side down in a baking dish. Reduce the syrup over high heat to 120 ml/4 fl oz/½ cup, spoon it over the apples and glaze them in the oven for about 20 minutes, turning them once and spooning syrup over them.

Mix the goose liver in a small bowl with the cream and remaining port. Fill the prunes with this paste, close them and set each prune in a glazed apple half.
Serves 4

KAAB EL GHZAL
GAZELLE'S HORNS

These North African sweet pastries are not strictly accompaniments to game, but they would make an amusing item at a meal in which game was served. You can use ready-made marzipan instead of the almond paste described here. Add a few drops of orange flower water and some cinnamon, but forget about the egg. However, the real effort in this recipe is kneading the pastry.

ALMOND PASTE:
250 g/8 oz/1⅓ cups blanched almonds
250 g/8 oz/1¼ cups caster sugar
a few drops of orange flower water
1 egg
1 teaspoon ground cinnamon

PASTRY:
300 g/10 oz/2 cups flour
150 g/5 oz/⅔ cup butter, melted, plus
more to grease baking sheet
a few drops of orange flower water

Combine the almonds, sugar and orange flower water, and grind them finely in a blender or food processor. Transfer to a bowl, mix in the egg and cinnamon and knead to a smooth paste.

Sift the flour a bowl, make a well in the centre and pour in the melted butter. Sprinkle in a little orange flower water, then stir the flour into the liquid. Make a stiff dough, adding a little water to get the right consistency. Knead this hard for a full half an hour (yes, 30 minutes!).

Preheat the oven to 180°C/350°F/gas 4. Divide the almond paste into 35 little lumps and form each into the shape of a rugby ball.

Divide the dough into 3 pieces. Roll out a piece on a floured board into a strip about 45 cm/18 in/18 in long and 7.5 cm/3 in/3 in wide. It will be very thin. Lay 12 pieces of almond paste lengthwise down the centre of the strips evenly spaced and not too close to the ends. Fold the sides of the strip over the top of the pieces of paste to make a long tube with lumps in it. Pinch the pastry inwards between the lumps – you are trying to get the appearance of a gazelle's horn. Cut the tube in half and lay the halves in a crescent shape on a buttered baking sheet. Repeat with the remaining almond paste and pastry. Bake for 15 to 20 minutes, or until nicely golden brown.

If you like, when the pastries are done and still hot, you can brush them with more orange flower water and sprinkle them with icing sugar.
Makes 6 large pastries

JERUSALEM ARTICHOKES AND WILD RICE STUFFING

This is suitable for most game birds.

250 g/8 oz/½ lb
   Jerusalem artichokes,
   chopped
1 medium onion,
   chopped

3 tablespoons butter
150 g/5 oz/2¾ cups
   cooked wild rice
   (cooked weight)
45 g/1½ oz/

3 tablespoons
   hazelnuts, toasted
   and chopped
4 tablespoons chopped
   fresh parsley

½ teaspoon summer
   savory
salt and black pepper
a little grated lemon zest

Sauté the artichokes and onion in the butter over a low heat for about 15 minutes. When they are just tender, add the wild rice and hazelnuts. Toss in the parsley, and savory, salt and pepper. Adjust the seasoning and stuff the birds.
Enough for 1 goose, or 3 pheasants

FENNEL SEED AND TARRAGON STUFFING

This has a faint liquorice perfume which goes very well with delicate birds such as quail, as well as with fish.

½ teaspoon fennel seeds
2 tablespoons fresh
   tarragon (or 1

teaspoon dried)
2 tablespoons chopped
   fresh parsley

6 tablespoons melted
   butter
about 175 g/6 oz/3 cups

roughly torn fresh
   breadcrumbs
salt and black pepper

Mix all the ingredients together.

Enough for about 8 quails.

RUSSIAN *KASHA* STUFFING

Kasha is buckwheat, and this Russian word is used elsewhere to describe hulled buckwheat used for making various dishes. Buckwheat is an important staple in Russia. Despite its appearance, it is not a cereal, but the seed of a plant of the same family as dock. It contains rutin, which is said to protect you against high blood pressure. When *kasha* is cooked, the texture should resemble that of properly cooked rice: not mushy, but with the grains soft and separate. It can be used instead of rice in any rice recipe, and can also be made into a porridge and served with honey and milk. Buckwheat flour makes the *gallettes* of Brittany and the *blinis* of Russia, and has a distinctive nutty flavour. It must be mixed with strong white flour to hold it together.

250 g/8 oz/heaped 1 cup kasha buckwheat
600 ml/1 pint/2½ cups water
2 teaspoons salt, and more as needed
1 tablespoon (or more)

butter, plus more for frying onion
1 medium onion, chopped
120 g/4 oz/1⅔ cups mushrooms, chopped
120 g/4 oz/1⅓ cups

cabbage, finely shredded
75 ml/2½ fl oz/⅓ cup vinegar
1 teaspoon tomato purée
2 cloves garlic, finely chopped

1 bay leaf, crumbled
120 ml/4 fl oz/½ cup stock
1 tablespoon sugar
black pepper

Wash the *kasha*. Add 2 teaspoons salt to the water, bring it to boiling point and add the *kasha*. Skim off any grains which float on the surface, add at least 1 tablespoon butter, and let this simmer until the liquid has been absorbed. Cover it tightly, and leave it to stand for 3 or 4 hours. There is a Russian saying, 'you can't spoil *kasha* with butter', and the more it absorbs the tastier it becomes (alas for those of us who have to worry about *la ligne*).

That is the basic method of cooking *kasha*, but to make a savoury stuffing, mix the cooked *kasha* with onions, to which you add the mushrooms and cabbage. When these have cooked and mixed together, raise the heat and add the vinegar, tomato purée, garlic, bay leaf and stock. Reduce, add the sugar and salt and pepper to taste, and let the liquid evaporate until the stuffing is fairly firm but not dry.
Enough for 1 large goose, or 4-6 pheasants

MOROCCAN COUSCOUS STUFFING

This is a stuffing which the Moroccans often use for a large piece of mutton, pot-roasted with onion, butter, honey, pepper, cinnamon and saffron. It would adapt perfectly to a big joint of venison cooked with or without these ingredients. It is also good for pigeon and chicken – though of course you will need much less stuffing for these.

1 kg/2 lb preprocessed couscous (see below)	300 g/10 oz/1¼ cups butter, melted	100 ml/3½ fl oz/⅓ cup orange flower water	400 g/13 oz/heaped 2 cups blanched, almonds
3 tablespoons oil	300 g/10 oz/1¼ cups caster sugar	500 g/1 lb/3⅓ cups seedless raisins	4 teaspoons ground cinnamon
1 tablespoon salt			

These instructions assume that you are using preprocess couscous. Unprocessed couscous is very laborious to prepare, and is best avoided. Put the couscous into a large bowl, cover with cold water and immediately drain it in a sieve. Tip it out on to a tray, spread it out and rub it with your hands to remove the lumps. Leave it for 20 minutes, during which you should rub it again several times. The last time, rub in 1 table-spoon oil.

The proper device for steaming couscous, a *couscoussière*, has very small holes in the base of the top part. A large ordinary steamer works perfectly well if you put a piece of muslin inside the top to cover the holes. Put plenty of water in the bottom of the steamer, fit on the top and set it to boil. When it is boiling briskly, sprinkle in a thin layer of couscous. When steam comes through this layer, add the rest of the couscous,

sprinkle on the salt and steam the couscous, covered, for 30 minutes.

Remove the steamer from the heat and let it stop steaming. Wearing oven gloves and taking care not to scald yourself, take off the top of the steamer and tip the couscous into the tray. As soon as you can touch it, rub it again. Add the melted butter, sugar and orange flower water and rub once more. Put the raisins in the water in the bottom of the steamer. Replace the top, tip in the couscous and steam it again for 20 minutes. Meanwhile, fry the almonds lightly in the re-maining oil, turning constantly until they are golden. Crush them coarsely.

When the couscous has finished steaming, tip it into a bowl, fluff it up with a fork and add the cooked raisins, crushed almonds and cinnamon. *Enough for 3-3½ kg/6-7 lb meat*

STUFFINGS FOR SALMON

These stuffings are ideal for a large piece of salmon, or any other firm-fleshed fish, wrapped in leaves and steamed. Use lettuce, spinach, Swiss chard, sorrel or vine leaves, and steam for about 25 minutes per 1 kg/2 lb; 12 minutes per 500g/1 lb. You can also steam the fish in foil, or bake it in pastry in an oven at 180°C/350°F/gas 4 for 35 minutes per 1 kg/2 lb; 15 minutes per 500g/1 lb.

FENNEL STUFFING:
Fennel has an aniseed taste. Slice the raw fennel bulb, sprinkle with a little salt and black pepper, and alternate wedges of fennel and lemon slices inside the cavity.

DILL STUFFING:
Combine fresh white breadcrumbs with finely chopped onion, finely chopped dill pickle, finely chopped sage, thyme, dill weed, salt and black pepper, and bind with melted butter and sour cream.

LEMON-ALMOND STUFFING:
Combine cooked rice with coarsely chopped blanched almonds, fresh parsley and tarragon, lemon juice and grated zest. Season with cayenne pepper, black pepper and salt, and bind with softened butter.

Allow about 100g/4 oz/¼ lb stuffing for 1 kg/2 lb fish; 45 g/1½ oz for 500 g/1 fish.

CRAB STUFFING FOR FISH

This is suitable for any fish. You can use frozen crab, but if you do, do not freeze the uncooked stuffing.

250 g/8 oz/½ lb fresh fish fillets, any sort	*chopped shallots*	*3 egg whites*	*250 g/8 oz/2 cups crab meat*
1 teaspoon finely	*1 teaspoon finely chopped parsley*	*3 tablespoons double cream (or sour cream)*	

Combine everything, little by little, in a blender, except the crab meat. Stir this in last.

Enough for a 5 kg/10 lb fish

BASIC SAUCE

This should be flavoured to suit the dish.

500 ml/16 fl oz/2 cups cooking liquid from a casserole, or stock
1 tablespoon cornflour
30 g/1 oz/2 tablespoons

butter, or 50 ml/1¾ fl oz/3⅓ tablespoons cream, sour cream, crème fraîche or yoghurt, or 2 egg

yolks
2 tablespoons chopped fresh herbs of your choice, or 50 g/1¾ oz/3⅓ tablespoons

prawns or puréed vegetables
salt and black or white pepper, as required.

Reduce the cooking liquid or stock to 250 ml/8 fl oz/1 cup. If you are flavouring the sauce with wine, add this and boil for a few minutes.
    Add the butter, cream, yoghurt or egg yolks.

Reheat the sauce gently. It must not boil again. Add any other flavourings, taste, and correct the seasoning.
Makes about 300 ml/10 fl oz/1¼ cups

BREAD SAUCE

This is a traditional accompaniment to roast pheasant and other birds.

300 ml/10 fl oz/1¼ cups milk, or more if necessary
30 g/1 oz/2 tablespoons

butter
1 medium onion, finely chopped
salt and white pepper

a little grated nutmeg
6 cloves
120 g/4 oz/2 cups fresh white breadcrumbs

1 tablespoon cream (optional)

Simmer all the ingredients except the bread-crumbs and cream. When the milk has been sufficiently infused with the flavour of cloves, fish these out, and stir in the breadcrumbs. Stir to

prevent it from sticking, and add more milk if the sauce becomes too thick. Add the cream at the last moment.
Makes 300-360 ml/10-12 fl oz/1¼-1½ cups

SHURA'S RUSSIAN CRANBERRY AND APPLE SAUCE

This can equally successfully be made with bilberries. It goes well with almost any game meats.

500 g/1 lb/5 cups cranberries	*sugar*	*juice and grated zest of ½ lemon*	*cooking apples, peeled, cored and*
500 g/1 lb/2½ cups	*1 bay leaf*	*750 g/1½ lb/6 cups*	*sliced*
	2 cloves		

Use a big, heavy saucepan. Pile in your berries, and about 500 ml/16 fl oz/2 cups water, and bring to the boil. When the berries start popping add the sugar, bay leaf, cloves and lemon juice and zest. Cook until the fruit mixture becomes thick, about 20 minutes.

Then add the apples and cook until they are *al dente*, not mushy, about 10 minutes more. Chill the sauce before sewing. Freezes well.
Makes about 1.5 l/2½ pints/6¼ cups

SALSA D'ACCHINGE
ANCHOVY SAUCE

This sauce is often served with boiled meat, but is a good accompaniment for any robust game or meat.

4 anchovy fillets	*1 clove of garlic*	*aboout 90 ml/3 fl oz/6 tablespoons olive oil*	*a little fresh mint, chopped (optional)*
1 tablespoon capers	*juice of ½ lemon*		

Chop the anchovies, capers and garlic. Add the lemon juice and enough olive oil to make a thick liquid. You can add a little mint if you like.
Makes about 100 ml/3½ fl oz/⅓ cup

GOOSEBERRY SAUCE

This sauce is perfect with goose and other rich meats, and also goes well with fish
– especially oily fish.

*250 g/8 oz/1²/₃ cups
  gooseberries
30 g/1 oz/2 tablespoons
  butter*

*2 tablespoons juices
  from the main dish
2 tablespoons crème
  fraîche or Greek-*

*style, thick yoghurt
a little sugar (optional)
a little grated nutmeg or*

*ground ginger
(optional)*

Cook the gooseberries gently in the butter until
soft, about 10 minutes. Sieve them. Return to
the pan and add the cooking liquid from the
game or fish the sauce is to accompany, and the
crème fraîche or yoghurt. Heat the sauce through
but do not let it boil. You can add a little sugar,
nutmeg or ginger if you like.
Makes about 100 ml/3½ fl oz/⅓ cup

SALSA GHIOTTA PER LA CACCIAGEONE
TARTY SAUCE FOR GAME

The cooking of Umbria is famous for its roasts, and especially for its wild game.
According to custom, game is cooked on a spit and while cooking it is
continuously brushed with a sauce kept underneath the roast in a pan.

*200 ml/7 fl oz/scant 1
  cup dry red wine
120 ml/4 fl oz/½ cup*

*olive oil
2 cloves garlic, chopped
1 anchovy fillet,*

*chopped
1 tablespoon capers,
  chopped*

*7 or 8 sage leaves
sprig of rosemary
salt and black pepper*

Mix all the ingredients and boil for a few
minutes to thicken the sauce slightly.
Makes about 360 ml/12 fl oz/1½ cups

SALSA AL TARTUFO
TRUFFLE SAUCE

The delicious black truffle found around Perugia in Umbria needs a little cooking in order to release the best of its aroma. This sauce is excellent on spaghetti, or with fish.

30 g/1 oz/1 oz black truffles

50 ml/1 ¾ fl oz/3⅓ tablespoons olive oil

1 anchovy fillet, chopped

Clean the truffles with a small brush, taking care not to break them. Wash, pat dry, and chop them very finely. Heat the olive oil in a small pan and add the chopped anchovy. Allow this to become creamy in consistency, but don't let it fry. Take the pan off the heat, add the truffles, mix well, and heat the sauce gently for just 1 minute more.

CHAMPAGNE SAUCE

This delicate sauce goes well with most kinds of fish.

1 bottle champagne
75 g/2½ oz/¾ cup shallots or spring onions, finely chopped

375 ml/12 fl oz/1½ cups fish stock
750 ml/1¼ pints/3 cups double cream
6 tablespoons butter

1 teaspoon chopped fresh basil, or tarragon, or dill (but not all together)
juice of ½ lemon

pinch of cayenne pepper or dash of Tabasco sauce
salt and black pepper

Cook the champagne and shallots or spring onions briskly until the liquid has reduced to about 45 ml/1½ fl oz/3 tablespoons. Add the fish stock and boil until slightly reduced again. Add the cream and simmer for about 10 minutes.

Lower the heat and add the butter, a little at a time, stirring with a wooden spoon until each piece dissolves before adding the next. When all the butter has been added, stir in the herbs, lemon juice and cayenne or Tabasco, and season to taste.

Makes about 1 l/1¾ pints/4 cups

FLORENTINE SHRIMP SAUCE

This sauce is adapted from a fourteenth-century recipe. The influence of the spice trade in this busy city is evident, as the taste is spicier than we are accustomed to expect from Italian dishes; indeed it is akin to something Indian. The mixture of egg yolks, oil and lemon juice make it an early version of mayonnaise. It works beautifully with any fish dish.

1 large slice of white bread, crust removed
120 ml/4 fl oz/½ cup milk
100 g/3½ oz shrimps,
cooked and shelled
5 blanched almonds
2 egg yolks
120 ml/4 fl oz/½ cup olive oil
½ teaspoon ground coriander
¼ teaspoon crushed fresh ginger
pinch of grated nutmeg
pinch of cayenne pepper
salt and black pepper
2 tablespoons lemon juice and ¼ teaspoon grated zest

Soak the bread in milk for 15 minutes.

Reserve a few shrimps to add to the sauce later. Grind or blend most of the shrimps with the almonds, then put them in a bowl. Squeeze the excess milk from the bread and add the bread to the mixture. Mix thoroughly. Stir in the egg yolks one at a time, stirring steadily, as when making mayonnaise, slowly add the olive oil, drop by drop, then the spices, salt and pepper. Finally add the lemon juice, drop by drop, and the zest, and at the end gently mix in the reserved shrimps.

SUMAC

When Afghans go hunting game they carry a little pouch of sumac. Often this is the only seasoning on the grilled meat. It is a spice the colour of dried blood, with a sour, tangy, lemony flavour. These days sumac can be bought in specialist food shops, and it is usually one of the condiments on the table in Lebanese and Persian restaurants. It is worth seeking out, for it is delicious on buttery rice. Persian *chelo kebab* would be unthinkable without raw egg yolk and sumac mixed through the buttered rice.

MARINADES

ORIENTAL MARINADE

This is excellent for duck.

*120 ml/4 fl oz/ ½ cup
 soy sauce
120 ml/4 fl oz/ ½ cup*

*sherry or port
120 ml/4 fl oz/ ½ cup
 olive oil*

*1 onion, chopped
1 tablespoon of grated
 fresh ginger*

*1 tablespoon of grated
 fresh tangerine or
 orange zest*

Mix the marinade ingredients well, then add the meat, turning from time to time to ensure an even absorbtion.

Enough for 1.5 kg/3 lb meat

MARINADE FOR WOOD PIGEONS

*400 ml/13 fl oz/1⅔
 cups dry red wine
1 tablespoon of olive oil
1 teaspoon of wine
 vinegar*

*1 tablespoon of crushed
 black pepper
6 whole cloves
2 cloves of garlic,
 crushed*

*5 bay leaves
2 juniper berries,
 crushed
1 sugar cube, saturated
 in brandy*

*a pinch each of dried
 rosemary, tarragon
 and dill*

Prepare as for Oriental Marinade.

Enough for 4 pigeons

WHITE WINE MARINADE

This is good for birds, especially pheasants.

300 ml/10 fl oz/1¼
   cups dry white wine
100 ml/3½ fl oz/⅓ cup
   white wine vinegar

2 teaspoons salt
1 tablespoon sugar
1 teaspoon dried thyme
2 bay leaves

5 whole colves
5 whole allspice berries
5 pink peppercorns,
   crushed

2 tablespoons olive oil
1 onion, chopped

Prepare as for Oriental Marinade.

Enough for 2 pheasants, or 4 smaller birds

JAPANESE TERIYAKI MARINADE

375 ml/12 fl oz/1½
   cups soy or tamari
   sauce

120 ml/4 fl oz/½ cup
   sake (sherry will do
   at a push)

6 tablespoons sugar
3 cloves of garlic,
   crushed

1 tablespoon crushed
   ginger, or ginger
   paste

Combine all of these ingredients and marinate the fish in the mixture for several hours, turning regularly.

Remove the fish from the marinade, and reserve this to use as an accompanying sauce. Grill the fish, basting several times with the marinade, and turning them. Undercook, rather than overcook. Heat the remaining marinade and pour it over the fish when you serve it.

Enough for 2 kg/4 lb fish

COOKED MARINADE

Use this for a saddle of venison or other large joints. This can be made in advance
and frozen for later use.

500 ml/16 fl oz/2 cups red wine	*375 ml/12 fl oz/1½ cups vinegar*	*1 clove of garlic, crushed*	*12-15 black peppercorns*
500 ml/16 fl oz/2 cups water	*2 onions, chopped*	*1 teaspoon dried thyme*	*1 tablespoon salt*
	1 carrot, sliced	*2 bay leaves*	
		4 sprigs of parsley	

Combine the ingredients and bring them to the
boil. Simmer for 1 hour. Let it cool before pouring over the meat.
Enough for 3½ kg/7 lb meat

STRONG MARINADE

This game marinade from my brother Michael in Kenya is guaranteed to tenderize
the toughest old beast. The key to this marinade is the lime juice, which is a classic
eastern tenderizer.

On safari meat is
normally barbecued or
grilled. Basil, which
grows wild in Africa, is
sometimes added to
marinades; and I have
heard of green coffee
beans being used as a
seasoning, but I have
been unable to obtain the
details.

10 cloves of garlic	*250 ml/8 fl oz/1 cup fresh lime juice*	*fresh tarragon*	*2 tablespoons of crushed black pepper*
1 tablespoon of salt	*1 tablespoon of chopped*	*1 small sweet red onion, chopped*	
1 bottle of dry red wine			

Cut 6 of the garlic cloves lengthwise into large
slivers. Stab the joint with a sharp knife and put
garlic pieces into the holes. Crush the remaining
garlic with the salt. Mix with the other ingredients together in a large bowl, pour over the
joint, and leave overnight in a cool place. If the
joint is not completely covered, turn every 4
hours. Use the marinade to baste when roasting,
and to make the gravy.
Enough for up to 3 kg/6 lb meat

DEALING WITH GAME

HANGING

Hot debate rages over this topic. In Britain and in Germany many people like a gamey flavour which ranges up the scale to very high. That is not so everywhere, and it should be a case for individual preference, not intimidation or even snobbery.

The effect of hanging is to allow the enzymes naturally present in the meat to break down its structure slightly, making it more tender. The enzymes also produce substances which give hung meat its characteristic flavour. Fish has much more powerful enzymes which spoil it quickly, which is why it should be as fresh as possible (the only exception being the sharks and rays, where a few days' storage allows the ammonia produced by the breakdown of protein to dissipate).

In Britain, game is hung in the following ways: birds, in feather and undrawn; hare and wild rabbit, furred and ungutted; deer or boar, gutted and bled before hanging. In America you are recommended to eviscerate everything immediately, and to tenderize by freezing. There are people who swear that birds should be hung by the head, others equally adamant that they should be hung by the feet. The same goes for animals. Farm-raised quail and hutch rabbits do not gain anything from hanging, and should be cooked straight away.

The advantage of cleaning and gutting immediately is that you will be able to identify any trace of abnormality or disease from examination of the abdominal cavity and liver. However, certain traditional dishes, such as woodcock, and a couple of Italian pigeon recipes I have included, specify that the innards should be left intact.

If you live in the city, hanging and cleaning will probably not concern you; it will be done before the game reaches your kitchen, unless kind friends drop off a brace straight from a weekend's shooting. If you are going to deal with game yourself, then a cold, airy place, where animals or birds can hang without touching each other, is necessary. If you hang anything by the feet, put a polythene bag round the head to prevent blood from dripping on to the floor. I check birds by testing the feathers above the tail. If they pull away softly, that is high enough for my palate.

Farmed venison will have been skinned before hanging; wild venison or venison bought from a game-dealer will most probably have been hung with the skin on. When it is hung with the skin on it is more difficult to butcher afterwards, but out of doors the skin protects the meat from insects and from drying out. Venison is eviscerated immediately after killing in order to allow the carcass to cool down as quickly as possible. It also makes it easier to transport.

It is important for all game that it should be able to cool quickly, and it is not advisable to leave birds, for instance, piled overnight in the back of a Land Rover, or heaped on a floor all touching each other. Hanging game birds undrawn and feathered helps to keep flies off, and it is tricky and messy to take the insides out without first plucking them.

FREEZING

There are two schools of thought about freezing game with, or without hanging first. I have read a number of American books and magazines where it is stated that freezing tenderizes meat and thus makes hanging unnecessary. However, hanging is not done solely to tenderize. Meat does become more tender as the enzymes break down its fibres, but that can also be achieved with marinades. The important point is that hanging strengthens the characteristic flavour of the meat and, given time, this changes from a subtle emphasis to a mature taste, finally becoming high. As far as I know, this natural change in flavour can only be achieved through hanging, and I prefer to freeze after hanging.

I have read glowing accounts of deer killed at the pre-dawn beginning of a day's hunt in the United States, which are skinned and cut up almost at once. When the hunter returns home at night, he unloads the car and puts the meat straight into the freezer. I have also seen American herb and spice packagers recommending instant freezing for tenderizing game. The action of freezing stretches and slightly disrupts the fibres as the water in the meat expands just before it freezes and through the formation of ice crystals. It does not, as far as my palate tells me, improve either the taste or the texture in a way comparable to hanging or marinating. Freezing is good for storage, it is convenient; but it is not a substitute for traditional methods.

The following procedures are best for freezing different kinds of game:

Birds should be plucked and the giblets removed (clean and freeze these separately, or else make giblet stock, which can also be frozen). Make sure the birds are cleaned thoroughly. Truss them ready for cooking, pad the legs with foil and wrap each bird completely in heavy-duty freezer polythene. Label it with weight, description and date. Pack jointed birds in portions, interspersed with greaseproof paper.

Hare and rabbit preferably should be hung before they are skinned and cleaned. Hutch rabbits need not be hung; these are best frozen in joints ready for cooking. Wrap and label as above.

Venison should be well hung before jointing and freezing like any other meat. Remove as much bone as possible so that it will take up less space in the freezer. Use the bones for stock. Wrap and label the joints. Venison can be stored frozen for up to 12 months; other game for an average of 6 months.

Fish should be frozen fresh and within 12 hours of being caught. The delicate flavour of salmon and trout can be maintained by freezing them in a sheet of ice. Clean the fish, then dip it several times in cold salted water (placing it on a tray in the freezer between immersions) so that a layer of ice forms round it and seals it from the air. Pack it in heavy-duty polythene, and label. You can cut the fish from frozen with a strong serrated knife.

PLUCKING AND DRAWING BIRDS

The first requirement is a draught-free space. In the case of the duck family, I keep my hands lightly oiled, this gives weight to the down as you pull it and helps to stop it floating unerringly upwards into your nose and hair, and if you were to sneeze while plucking a bird the result would be a disastrous mess. I pluck inside a large pillowcase or plastic bag pinned to my lap. A light, smooth action is required, so that you don't tear the skin. Feathers are easily removed from birds which have been hung. I start with the breast, then move on to the sides, back, legs and wings. Wing feathers can be tough: hold the wing taut with one hand, then tug in the direction of the feather's growth. If necessary, use pliers to pull them out.

After you have plucked the bird, singe it over a naked gas flame so that all the fine hair-like feathers and the little bits you can't quite get out are burnt off. Trim the legs and wings as you wish. Cut off the bird's head, turn the bird on its side and use a little sharp knife to slit the skin of the neck to the shoulders. Peel back the skin to expose the neck, and cut this where it joins the body. Reserve this piece of neck for stock, which you will make with the giblets, and later with the carcass and bones.

Wiggle your finger inside the neck cavity to loosen the windpipe and gullet, which feel like slightly ridged plastic tubing. Gently pull these. The crop will come away with them. Cut the crop open, and pull the inner lining and the contents of the crop, which will show what the bird has been eating. Discard these, but keep the outside of the crop for the stock you will make. Turn the bird and pinch the skin below the end of the breastbone, pulling this out slightly, then use the little sharp knife to make a cut just above the vent, big enough to insert your finger. Gently run your finger round the abdominal cavity, next to the bone, to release the innards. You should be able to pull these out in one mass. Keep the heart and liver. Cut out of the liver the greenish gall bladder section, taking a little more than you might think necessary to ensure that none of these bitter-tasting parts remain. Wood pigeons have no gall bladder. When cleaning a duck you must remove the oil glands, which are two little lumps on the upper side of the bird's tail. Wash and dry the bird, and you are ready for the next stage.

Some birds, such as mergansers (fish-eating ducks) should be skinned rather than plucked to reduce their fishy taste. Tie a string around the bird's neck, hang it up, slit the skin down the breast and peel it off. In some parts of the world, these fishy-tasting fowl are cooked as fish, another way of dealing with it.

Small birds can be split and flattened for sautéing or grilling. After plucking cut off the head, feet and wingtips. Use sharp kitchen scissors to split the bird lengthwise, cutting along the backbone from the tail to the neck. Remove the innards and flatten the bird by pressing on a hard surface with the palm of your hand over the breast. Make a slit in the flap of skin between the bird's legs, bend the legs inwards, and slip them through this flap, side by side.

Pellets of shot should be removed when possible. Use the end of a sharp-pointed knife to apply pressure, and pop them out. A bird which is badly shot is better cooked in a casserole, after you cut away any flesh which is too badly bruised or damaged ever to taste good.

SKINNING AND GUTTING SMALL FURRED GAME
In the U.S.A. there are a number of small furry animals which are eaten with quite a degree of enthusiasm. These include porcupine, muskrat, beaver, woodchuck, raccoon, opossum and squirrel, as well as rabbit and jackrabbit – the American term for hare. Except for rabbit, hare, porcupine and squirrel, all of these have glands, found in the armpits and along the spine towards the tail, which must be removed before any further preparation takes place. These animals can be cooked in various ways; any of the rabbit recipes in this book can be used for them.

TO PREPARE A RABBIT
Although porcupine and opossum require a bit of special attention, small animals are dealt with in much the same way, so I will use rabbit as my example.

Nick the skin around the ankles of the hind legs, then make lengthwise cuts along the inside of the leg and thigh to the base of the tail, taking care to cut no deeper than the skin. Slit the skin from the base of the tail along the belly, being careful not to puncture the abdominal cavity. Go as far as the neck. Then firmly but gently peel the skin off in the same directions as you have cut. It will come off like a neat glove if you are patiently persistent. Do the same around the forelegs, then pull the skin over the head and cut off the head and the skin where you have decided to

stop. In certain recipes, such as braised hare, the head is skinned but left attached. To do this you must cut off the ears at the base, cut the skin carefully around the eyes and mouth, and the rest of the skin will peel away. The liver is just below the rib cage and quite delicate. Remove it carefully, and cut away the gall bladder, which is of a greenish colour. Cut away a little more than just this greenish part, because it is important not to include any of this bitter-tasting tissue. Be very careful not to puncture the gall bladder as you cut. Discard this with the intestines and paws.

In making jugged hare the blood is the vital ingredient in the sauce. To release the blood from the chest cavity, hold the animal over the bowl and slit the base of the chest with the tip of a sharp knife. When you have collected the blood, remove the heart and lungs. These can be used in a stuffing. Trim away the ends of the windpipe and oesophagus.

If the liver of any animal or bird is swollen, and has light-coloured lumps on it about the size of a matchhead, dispose of the whole carcass immediately, as it is diseased. Don't even feed it to your dog, and be careful to wash your hands and all utensils extremely well.

CLEANING AND FILLETING FISH
The fresher the fish, the better it tastes, ideally, off the hook, cleaned and then straight into the waiting pan.

With a sharp knife (or kitchen scissors) cut along the belly from the vent up to the head. Pull out the guts, and then scrape out the soft, dark blood-coloured vein-like structure (which is the fish's kidney) that lies along the backbone. The best tool for doing this is a human thumb, but use a knife if you prefer. Wash the fish.

If you have a small fish like a trout, and intend to cook it in a pan with butter, herbs, almonds, or whatever, then you may wish to leave the head on. In that case, having gutted and cleaned the fish, as outlined above, you are ready to cook it. Easy, isn't it?

If you decide to fillet the fish, there are a few more things to do. Salmon and trout are very considerate about the way their bones are placed. After gutting, cut off the head and tail, then cut along the spine from the inside, keeping the point of the knife well down on to the back-bone. Pull out the spine through this incision. If any flesh sticks to the spine, ease it gently back.

Alternatively, after gutting the fish and cutting off the head and tail, cut along the backbone from the other side, removing the dorsal fin as you proceed. Cut the fillets off the ribs by running a knife up from the tail end, keeping it flat against the bones, and repeat on the other side.

To skin the fillets, cut out the fins, then take a flat-bladed knife and ease it between the skin and flesh. Carry on doing this, holding the flesh down firmly as you ease skin and flesh apart.

GLOSSARY

American measures are given with each recipe after the metric and Imperial weights. This is a glossary of ingredients and cookery terms American cooks may be unfamiliar with.

GAME

Blackcock: a male Black grouse
Capercaillie: a member of the grouse family
Ptarmigan: a member of the grouse family found in cold, dry regions, especially Alaska

INGREDIENTS

Bacon rashers: bacon slices
Black pudding: blood sausage
Broad beans: substitute lima beans
Cider: hard cider
Cornflour: cornstarch
Courgettes: zucchini
Court bouillon: bouillon for cooking fish
Cream, double or thick: heavy
Cream, single: light
Flour, plain or strong: all-purpose
Flour, wholemeal: wholewheat
Globe artichokes: artichokes
Mangetouts: snow peas
Meaux mustard stoneground mustard
Pine kernels: pine nuts
Potted shrimps small shrimps preserved in clarified butter; sold in small jars in England

Prawns: shrimp
Rowan jelly: a jelly made from the tart red berries of the Mountain Ash. A traditional accompaniment to venison, but beech plum jelly would be an appropriate substitute
Spring onions: scallions
Sugar, caster: superfine
Sugar, icing: confectioners
Sultanas: golden raisins
Tomato purée: tomato paste
vine leaves: grape leaves

COOKERY TERMS AND EQUIPMENT

Baking foil: aluminium foil
Clingfilm: plastic wrap
Frying pan: skillet
Greaseproof paper: use waxed paper
To grill: to broil unless it is outdoors on a barbecue
Loaf tin: loaf pan
Muslin: cheesecloth
Roasting tin: roasting pan
Stoned: pitted
Tinned: canned

INDEX